THE NOBLE AGENT'S GUIDE TO LEVEL FUNDING

HOW TO BUILD A GOOD LIFE SERVING AMERICAN SMALL-BUSINESS HEALTH PLANS

THOMAS STEIN

Legal Disclaimer

The information provided in this book about Level Funding is for general educational and informational purposes only. While Level Funding can offer potential benefits to some employers, it is a complex topic that requires careful consideration and expert guidance. This book is not intended to serve as legal, financial, or insurance advice.

Level Funding involves intricate regulations under the Employee Retirement Income Security Act (ERISA) and carries significant fiduciary responsibilities for employers. Subsequent changes in applicable law may impact the content of this book.

Before considering or implementing a Level Funded plan, employers should consult with qualified legal counsel, financial advisors, and insurance professionals who specialize in ERISA and self-funded health plans.

The author is not responsible for any actions (or liability for any errors or omissions) taken based on the information presented in this book. As the information contained within this book does not constitute legal, financial, or insurance advice, it should never be used without first consulting with a professional to determine what may best suit the needs of the employer. Readers are strongly encouraged to seek professional advice tailored to their specific circumstances before making any decisions regarding health insurance plans.

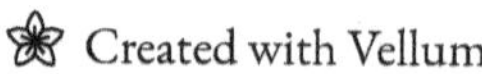 Created with Vellum

To my Family

To my parents, who taught me the art of thinking and the roots from which we have grown, anchoring me in the wisdom of the past.
To my wife, whose unwavering support has nurtured an idealistic young man into a person of value and purpose.
To my sons, who remind me daily of the significance of our family name, teaching me that we are merely stewards of this legacy, guiding it forward.

May this work be a beacon to the future, illuminating a path strong enough for the next generation to carve their own Noble way.

There is a misperception that the market only rewards the Machiavellian. This could not be further from the truth. If the young, noble broker is willing to spend the time developing his Book of Business and serve the clients that he wants to go through life with, then life can be very good and rewarding for all involved. Find out just how rewarding with the Great Life Calculator.

Contents

Introduction: The Noble Agent's Guide to Level Funding

"Insurance is the lucky many paying for the unlucky few."

In the competitive world of health insurance sales, it's easy for young agents to get caught up in the daily grind of prospecting, quoting, and closing deals. But amidst the hustle, it's crucial to remember the deeper purpose behind your work. Selling health insurance isn't just about making a living—it's an opportunity to build a rewarding career, help your clients' businesses thrive, and make a positive impact on the lives of hard-working Americans.

As you navigate the challenges of building your own book of business, it's important to focus on cultivating meaningful relationships with your clients, not just chasing quick sales. By challenging common assumptions and bringing innovative ideas to the table, you can earn the trust and respect of small business owners desperate for a better way.

This book provides a blueprint for evolving from a spreadsheet jockey to a specialized advisor. It maps out strategies for relatively new agents getting into the competitive world of selling health insurance plans, with a focus on gaining expertise in the innovative solution called Level Funding. Level Funding allows many small businesses with under 100 employees to take control of their healthcare costs and potentially receive money back at the end of the year.

Level Funding isn't a new concept—my father was doing it before me, but many people in the industry haven't heard about it because it isn't promoted by major carriers. It's an established approach that has been around for decades, blending elements of self-insurance and stop loss coverage. By tailoring plans to the unique needs of smaller groups, Level Funding empowers businesses to operate like their own mini-insurance companies. They can retain control over unused claims dollars that would normally pad the wallets of big, fully-insured corporate carriers.

Throughout this book, we'll explore the biggest pitfalls new agents face, from the temptation to cut corners for quick commissions to the fear of pushing back on client demands. We'll outline proven strategies for overcoming these hurdles and building a sustainable, rewarding practice grounded in specialist knowledge and trust.

You'll learn how to secure verbal commitments from prospects, even in the face of skepticism or pushback. We'll discuss how to find hidden gems in overlooked market niches and convert them into profitable, long-term clients. And most importantly, we'll emphasize the importance of playing the long game—prioritizing client success over short-term wins.

While mastering Level Funding requires more legwork than traditional fully insured plans, the payoff for this extra effort is immense. You'll transform from a transactional vendor to an indispensable strategic partner, building a loyal client base that values your expertise and ability to drive results. With a knowledge of level funded plans, you can build unshakable trust and incredible career stability. Let's get started.

Don't Be a Spreadsheeter

"It is a crime to take your work less than seriously."
— Unknown

Brad was the stereotypical Spreadsheeter—all he cared about were the numbers on the rate sheet in front of him. I met him at a networking event when I had just started selling health plan services to small businesses. Eager to bring new clients onto the books, I began my well-rehearsed pitch about the value of crafting customized plans. But before I could even finish my opening line, Brad cut me off. "What are your rates?" he barked, staring intently at his spreadsheet. "I've got Big Carrier at $320 per employee per month, Huge Fella at $340, and Massive Company at $360. If you can beat those numbers, I can send some quotes your way. If not, I'm not interested."

Taken aback, all I could mutter was, "Well, our rates depend on the group's unique factors..." Before I could explain further why a tailored approach matters, Brad was already walking away. "Don't waste my time!" he scoffed. "Just focus on the bottom line."

That interaction helped me realize how health insurance agents often fail by doing nothing to differentiate themselves beyond relaying current premium rates. They think their value comes from accessing the best prices on commoditized corporate plans. But the clients themselves could do this, using an online quoting tool that spits out a list of rates. This approach borders on insulting. The methodology is transactional rather than consultative. Even worse, it makes brokers easily replaceable—they are like homes in a development where every house looks the same.

In the early days of my career, I was like Brad. Maybe not as standoffish, but as a Green Horn (a term we use for rookies in the business) I struggled to differentiate myself from the competition. Like most newcomers, I relied on rate comparisons to make sales. I thought my job was about comparing numbers. But after banging my head on closed doors for months, I realized being a spreadsheet minion was a dead-end path, both financially and fulfillment-wise.

There I was with my neat grid of rates from different plans, explaining deductibles to prospects who quickly glazed over with boredom. The other Green Horns all had the same spreadsheets. As far as the clients were concerned, we were totally replaceable. Why should they buy from me instead of someone else offering the exact same coverage for 0.2% less? I had fallen into the trap of commoditization— competing purely on price instead of value.

The harsh reality of those early months nearly broke me. As I slogged through my call sheets fruitlessly, my desperation grew. I lacked any nuance in my pitch beyond reciting numbers off my comparison charts, mechanically running prospects through the same sequence of generic sales questions. Without a compelling reason for business owners to switch plans, my close rate stalled near zero. My bank account dwindled as my dreams of easy success evaporated. Bouncing between frustration and panic, I struggled to understand where I'd gone wrong. Why did the tricks that had fired up my initial enthusiasm eventually flame out and die? Why did assured promises from managers gradually begin to ring hollow? How had I fooled myself into believing health insurance would be simple? Or that reaching six figures was just a matter of hustling hard enough?

The answer took time to surface. But when I finally stopped flailing long enough to assess my situation with clarity, the reason for my failure was obvious. I had become a Spreadsheeter—one of the countless minions relying on price comparisons alone, oblivious to the deeper complexities of the health insurance industry. Spreadsheeters treat all available health plans as generic commodities, assuming minor differences in deductibles or premiums are sufficient to make a sale. They push whichever product offers the best commission bump, ignoring larger implications. They serve their own bottom lines first, giving clients only as much detail as needed for a signature.

My process was faulty, yet complaints from prospects consistently centered on cost. When they said my prices were too high, I dropped the rates lower, giving away my commission until entire days were wasted pitching low-margin plans—anything to clinch a sale. I became a short order cook desperately offering cheaper meals, unaware the client had ordered something else entirely, off the menu I never let them see.

My confidence eroded. I hardly valued my own time and effort, scrambling to work for free, chasing unlikely deals that never paid off. Worse, my need for commission blinded me to my clients' needs. I ignored relationship-building, focusing narrowly on overcoming objections around premium costs. I assumed clients would switch to me only if my plan was slightly cheaper than their existing one. With no compelling differentiator beyond the premium rate itself, I was doomed to fight on price alone. As any good negotiator knows, when you only have one point of leverage, there will only be one winner.

The turning point came when I lost a big prospect to a competitor who offered barely lower rates. I had invested hours researching their needs, customizing a proposal, and discussing cost-saving strategies. But in the end, all the client cared about was saving a few bucks. As I sulked back to my rented compact car, empty Starbucks cup in hand instead of a signed offer, I knew something had to change. I couldn't go on being a Spreadsheeter. If the only ground I fought on was price, then I was bound to lose.

That's when I realized the insurance agents who thrive over the long-term don't compete on price. They offer value beyond rates. They establish trust by solving problems through specialization. The best brokers evolve into consultants—or Main Street Mavericks—for their clients. They put in the work to understand specific needs, provide tailored solutions, and make themselves indispensable.

I decided if I was going to make it in this ruthlessly competitive business, I had to differentiate myself from the spreadsheet-pushing pack. My father, Tom Stein Sr., is an industry legend. He had been doing this for decades with great success. But I was determined to make it on my own, without having to ask for his help. I wanted to do it myself.

But then I kept banging my head against the wall and hitting dead ends. Eventually, I caved and asked my dad for advice. That's when I first learned about an uncommon offering called Level Funding. Dad sent me to shadow one of our biggest superstar agents for a week. I noticed this guy was doing just about everything differently from the rookie agents I was around all day. So I started implementing what I saw and the results were awesome.

I developed expertise around Level Funding plans. I learned how to translate complex ideas about self-funding, stop loss, and reference-based pricing into simple concepts business owners could grasp. I mastered the mechanics of underwriting and building plans specially designed around my clients' risk profiles.

Most importantly, I focused on building trust instead of chasing transactions. I invested time upfront demonstrating my knowledge. And I emphasized relationship-building over pushing for quick sales. I realized, in the immortal words of Theodore Roosevelt, that "people don't care how much you know until they know how much you care."

This approach was the opposite of Hollywood-ized high-pressure sales tactics. Instead of overwhelming clients with urgent calls to action, I patiently earned credibility. I set myself apart as an expert guide who could navigate the tangled web of regulations to create stability amid healthcare complexities. I refused to be just another sales rep hungry for commissions. When I redefined my role to become an indispensable advocate in the quest for employee retention, clients responded. As a trusted advisor with specialized knowledge, I earned business through expertise instead of competing solely on rates. The flood of referrals spoke for itself.

My choice to reject spreadsheeting in favor of differentiation changed everything. The pitfalls of relying solely on spreadsheet analysis are becoming increasingly apparent as A.I.-based quoting tools have become commonplace in the market. Prevailing as a Spreadsheeter becomes less plausible each passing year.

So, how do we evolve the broker role beyond a commoditized quoting engine into a specialized expert? The solution lies in transitioning from price peddling to dynamic relationship building. You need to evolve from a Spreadsheeter to a Main Street Maverick.

What is a Main Street Maverick?

"Slow is smooth and smooth is fast."
— *Navy SEALs*

Becoming a Main Street Maverick rather than a Spreadsheeter requires transitioning from a transactional sales approach to a consultative one. Your focus must be on solving clients' deeper business challenges. This means going beyond reciting insurance rates to diagnose underlying issues and craft customized solutions.

Main Street Mavericks have invested their time into bringing the best, not just the cheapest, programs to their clients. They serve as prescribers of solutions, not dictators of numbers. Jumping to pitch offerings too quickly diminishes not only credibility, but professionalism. Meaningless numbers insult the very customer they are meant to serve. But if Main Street Mavericks offer anything, it is a meaningful solution.

Meaningful solutions require a deep understanding of a business and its problems.

In the 1970s, Xerox had a leader in Cleveland who took over an office that wasn't doing well. At the time, Xerox salespeople were told to spend as little time as possible with customers after delivering new copiers. They were taught to install the machines quickly and then move on to the next customer. Ironically, this approach made Cleveland one of the worst sales territories.

So, Corporate sent in a new chief to the shop, and he had a different set of ideas. The new Cleveland chief ordered his team to spend hours with clients asking questions, observing workflows, and identifying major pain points. Instead of immediately leaving after equipment delivery, reps immersed themselves in each company's operations, shadowing employees and suggesting process improvements.

The results were remarkable. Client retention shot through the roof. What's more notable is that while this strategy focused on trust-building above short-term sales, the team far exceeded their revenue targets. Although counterintuitive, the approach centered on understanding and adding value instead of pushing to close more deals. And that made all the difference to cementing relationships beyond one-off transactions.

When selling health insurance, Spreadsheeters view sales as a numbers game won through clever tricks or aggression. It's a rather myopic viewpoint. They believe their offerings are intrinsically valuable on features alone. But Main Street Mavericks recognize long-term success requires specialization and empathy alongside drive and competence. They provide educational support to guide clients on an ongoing journey rather than just pushing to complete a transaction.

This example contains the essence of the Main Street Maverick's model. Like the Cleveland Xerox team, health insurance brokers must investigate beyond surface issues to uncover business difficulties at a deeper level. A good agent asks probing questions, listens attentively to identify unseen obstacles, then prescribes relevant solutions that can't be found on a spreadsheet. This elevates client perceptions of the broker as an indispensable expert rather than replaceable salesperson.

Becoming a Main Street Maverick requires both mindset and activity shifts. It means embracing ambiguity, avoiding assumptions, and investing time to comprehend challenges from the client's perspective before proposing any products. Only after defining the true problem can you determine appropriate solutions. Jumping to pitch offerings too quickly diminishes credibility. Effective brokers first establish themselves by understanding the client's circumstances better than anyone else. This makes the broker less vulnerable to replacement by competitors who focus solely on premium rates or features.

This conceptual shift from product-pusher to problem-solver reframes the broker role around trust rather than efficiency or scale. Main Street Mavericks invest significant effort to understand the client's worldview. The payoff is that they can translate complex ideas into compelling visions for the future. They make concepts like level-funding and reference-based pricing feel accessible by using relatable language, helpful metaphors, and clear illustrations. They turn intimidating regulations into navigable guidelines through meticulous communication.

To compete in chaotic conditions, establishing trust must be every broker's priority. With rising expenses, regulatory shifts, and technology disruption perpetually on the horizon, the health insurance industry grows more turbulent each year. Clients seek advisors they can depend on. As the Cleveland Xerox team discovered, this counterintuitive path ultimately yields the strongest growth and retention if executed diligently over time.

Becoming indispensable means going narrow and deep rather than wide and shallow. Main Street Mavericks win trust by asking smart questions. Prescribing tailored solutions cements loyalty beyond pricing. Serve specific needs over selling generic products. Deliver extreme value. This is the road to a long and prosperous career.

The key difference between Spreadsheeters and Main Street Mavericks boils down to mindset. Spreadsheeters believe their differential value lies in accessing the best rates. Main Street Mavericks rely on knowledge and wisdom accrued from experience to uncover optimal solutions. Both follow systematic approaches, but while Spreadsheeters input superficial variables into simplified quoting tools designed for standardization, Main Street Mavericks painstakingly collect details through discovery practices focused on customization.

For example, a construction company might cite cost savings as their primary objective. But upon further discussion, it becomes clear their main aims center on attracting and retaining skilled workers in a competitive hiring market. The cost of turnover in this industry is thousands of dollars per employee. Armed with this insight, the broker can tailor recommendations around boosting recruitment and retention through enhanced benefits rather than just reducing premiums.

Becoming a Main Street Maverick requires mastering both left-brain and right-brain selling. Left-brain selling relies on spreadsheets—it is logical, analytical, and data-driven. In contrast, right-brain selling prioritizes vision, relationship building, and emotional connectivity. Excellent brokers blend both approaches seamlessly. Left-brain selling makes the business case for switching plans based on measurable ROI. Right-brain selling envisions an improved future centered around employee wellbeing. Together, they make change seem both financially prudent and emotionally aligned.

Transitioning beyond the role of annoying product peddler to position yourself as an indispensable expert is no easy task. This level of change seldom unfolds without determined effort. But rejecting rote selling techniques in favor of bespoke solutions ensures you can offer irreplaceable value. Your defender against commoditization becomes comprehensive knowledge itself.

The next step involves translating consultative principles into action. This requires grasping exactly why tailored benefit plans build lasting success compared to one-size-fits all alternatives—and what it looks like in application. And that's where Level Funding enters the picture.

Building Trust Through Level Funding

"Without trust, nothing moves."
— *Charlie Munger*

The secret ingredient that supercharges results for Main Street Mavericks in the health insurance world is a product called Level-Funded Health Insurance. Level Funding allows companies to self-insure health plans while managing risk. Employers pay fixed monthly amounts to fund expected claims, administration fees, and stop loss. At the end of the year if employees used less care than projected, the surplus of the claims fund is returned to the plan owner. This transforms health benefits from a pure expense into a value-driving asset.

It's as if your apartment building created its own mini-insurance company. All the tenants agree to pay monthly fees into a pool. Then, whenever anyone has a leaky pipe, they can make a claim and it gets paid from the communal pot. If there's cash left over after paying out all the claims at the end of the year, it is divided up and everyone gets a refund check!

Continuing with this analogy, imagine your apartment's mini-insurance plan also had a team of professional underwriters to carefully evaluate the likelihood of each unit needing repairs, so you could accurately calculate appropriate premiums based on known risks. Then throw in a feature known as stop loss coverage from a commercial insurer, which would protect the pool from any individual tenant having a gazillion-dollar problem that busts the budget, like a burst pipe that floods their whole living room.

In this scenario, the incentive alignments are beautiful—the better your fellow tenants all take care of their apartments, the more cash potentially comes back to you. Suddenly you start wanting to help your neighbors out with home improvement projects instead of resenting them for asking you to check on their place while they are on vacation!

Level Funding introduces similar motivations around workplace wellness. Plans reduce realized cost when their employees use preventative care and avoid expensive procedures. The business is incentivized to promote healthy lifestyles. It's no longer just about paying lip service to "employee wellness initiatives." Everybody wins when employees are healthier.

This flips the traditional script of viewing insurance purely as an unavoidable expense. In fact, over the past decade, I've seen tens of millions of dollars in surplus checks returned to ecstatic clients who never dreamed such a thing was possible. They've used these surplus funds to reduce their healthcare costs, allowing them to invest in new equipment, hire more staff, take team vacations, and expand facilities. Not only does Level Funding lower costs through superior underwriting, it transforms benefits spending into a strategic growth driver when those extra dollars get used to catalyze business expansion.

By returning surplus claim funds to clients, Level Funding realigns broker interests with policyholders. No longer are advisors incentivized to sell generic plans focused on maximizing earnings for insurance company shareholders. Instead, they are motivated to meticulously track healthcare utilization so they can send unspent claims funding back at the end of each year. The refund potential changes the rules of the game.

The shared upside of Level Funding creates the accountability that is lacking in traditional health insurance plans. Fully insured policies essentially protect employers from having to think about care consumption consequences, with insurers assuming all financial risks. But this also divorces clients from all rewards. In effect, traditional plans "numb" decision makers from feeling the full impact of their healthcare choices. In contrast, Level Funding "wakes up" leadership by making everyone partners in achieving gains that translate into actual surplus dollars at the end of the year.

That heightened accountability fuels better consumer behaviors that bend cost curves lower. When employees recognize that all their colleagues directly benefit from well-managed health plans, they become more conscientious regarding discretionary spending on services. Furthermore, heightened awareness of financial waste on health insurance often sparks dialogues around stewardship, potentially translating into lifestyle decisions that reduce risks amongst workers (like going to the doctor for normal care instead of the emergency room).

What do I mean by "financial waste"? Milton Friedman's famous "four types of money" thought experiment perfectly illustrates this concept. As the title suggests, there are four types of money:

- **Type-1 Money:** Your own money that you spend on yourself.
- **Type-2 Money:** Someone else's money that you spend on yourself.
- **Type-3 Money:** Your own money that you spend on someone else.
- **Type-4 Money:** Someone else's money that you spend on another person.

Imagine you and a sales prospect go out to dinner. If you're spending your own money on yourself, you'll likely be quite prudent in your choices, carefully considering the cost and quality of each item. But if your prospect is covering the meal then you might not think twice about the price of your main. The incentives are misaligned.

Now consider the third scenario—you're spending your own money on someone else, like when you're personally picking up the tab for the table. Here you'll still aim for quality because you don't want your prospect to think you're cheap, but you will be more price-sensitive than in the second scenario. Finally, there is the scenario that all sales people crave and far too many companies indulge: the one where you are spending someone else's money on someone else. Wining and dining. Five course steak dinners with decadent mini-cake desserts. Sure, you might close the deal, but it is objectively the least economical use of anyone's dollars.

This phenomenon is not limited to sales. Anytime someone is spending someone else's money on a third party, they have the least incentive to economize or maximize value. The further removed the spender is from the money's source and ultimate beneficiary, the less judicious they'll be. This is true for kids who receive gift cards from distant relatives on their birthdays, and for governments that spend east coast taxpayer dollars on west coast problems.

The universe of health insurance plans is no exception. Members of fully-insured plans are essentially buying into a near-infinite pool of claims dollars they can spend quite liberally. While there is no consequence for submitting claims that are maybe not super necessary, there is also no reward for staying healthy and not submitting claims. Consequently, members feel like they have a use-it-or-lose-it deal and then end up using *all of it* (and then some). However, the money must come from somewhere, and so year-over-year most companies see their premiums rise.

Level Funding fosters a collaborative partnership between employers and employees by equally involving them in the pursuit of efficiency improvements. The direct conversion of gains into larger benefits budgets contrasts with traditional models that create a detached and disinterested attitude toward benefits as a mere operating cost. This misalignment often leads to resentment and mistrust between management and staff due to perceived overspending or indifference to worker needs. Level Funding addresses these conflicts by aligning leaders as equal partners in achieving efficiency gains that directly translate into expanded benefits budgets. This shared goal eliminates arguments that can manifest as cultural tension or operational inefficiencies, resulting in a unified pursuit of improved outcomes for both parties.

Refunding surplus money directly back to plan sponsors builds an immense level of trust, which is essential in health insurance sales. Clients seek partners who can provide guidance and navigate complex markets with integrity and transparency. Level Funding is the special sauce that allows agents to provide smaller businesses with an ideal combination of affordability, flexibility, and strategic control. Blending self-insurance with stop loss protection, this model puts clients in the driver's seat of plan design, claims management, and refund potential.

For brokers selling traditional plans, transitioning to a niche specialty like Level Funding involves more upfront effort. They must educate themselves extensively on self-insurance regulations for small employers and the complexities of stop loss arrangements before even attempting to pitch these offerings. They need to intimately understand contracts between third party administrators (TPAs) and stop loss providers. They endure trial and error determining optimal stop loss attachment points per client.

In other words, there's no shortcut. Before deploying Level Funding successfully, you're going to have to roll up your sleeves and perform extensive research and tests. Half-baked attempts often backfire due to the delicate balancing act required. But brokers willing to specialize can gain a formidable edge in connecting smaller groups with customized plans.

The key is combining unwavering diligence with an entrepreneurial spirit, and a commitment to keep innovating regardless of hurdles. As daunting as this sounds initially, every great journey begins with a first step. Whether you're a spreadsheet jockey seeking differentiation or an established broker battling disenchantment, it's never too late to expand capabilities. The world always needs more Davids slaying Goliaths. Level Funding hands innovative brokers the stones they need to strike at the heart of corporate hegemony. All it takes is a willingness to stand apart from rigid norms and unleash daring ideas.

EMBRACING LEVEL FUNDING AS YOUR DIFFERENTIATOR

"The man who says he can and the man who says he can't are both usually right."
— *Henry Ford*

In an industry flooded with generic corporate plans, Level Funding provides a way for brokers to offer clients something truly unique and valuable. However, many established agents remain skeptical that Level Funding works for small groups under 100 employees. These misconceptions present an opportunity for new agents willing to embrace this innovative model.

The power of Level Funding as a differentiator was cemented for me in my early career when I received an unexpected phone call. It was from a delighted small business owner I'd partnered with the previous year. "Tom, you're not going to believe this!" he exclaimed. "We just got a refund check in the mail for $58,000! I never imagined we'd see this kind of money back from our health insurance plan. You've got my business for life, sir."

I was thrilled, but also surprised. While I was confident in Level Funding's potential, this was another piece of proof that the concept could deliver long-term value for my clients. It was one thing to theoretically talk about surplus return potential during sales meetings. But now I could point to real-world examples of five-figure windfalls landing in my clients' hands.

Over my next few annual renewals, success stories like this one multiplied. Another employer used their $32,000 return to reduce healthcare spending, allowing them to invest in a much-needed expansion of their machine shop. This positioned them to keep manufacturing operations from moving overseas. A family-owned restaurant used their $18,000 surplus to finally afford adding dental insurance for employees after a decade without coverage. The founders of a struggling physical therapy startup credited Level Funding surpluses for keeping their business afloat through early growing pains.

Of course, Level Funding isn't some magical financial scheme guaranteeing effortless payouts. Constructing these self-funded plans requires extensive understanding of employers' needs, meticulously projecting employee healthcare risks, shrewdly balancing stop loss arrangements, and patiently guiding owners into a model they haven't considered before. You will endure growing pains as you illuminate customers of Level Funding's merits.

I recently worked with a small manufacturing company, and that process illustrates the many twists and turns these deals can take on the way to the first surplus check. Let's call them ABC Fabricators (not their real name, I changed all company names BTW), a metal fabrication shop with thirty-two employees. As a newer company, they were struggling to offer health benefits while keeping costs contained. Their original fully insured plan was getting more expensive by the year, and employees were paying ever-higher deductibles for the same coverage. Morale was sinking as fast as renewal rates were rising.

After an extensive consultation during their open enrollment period, their broker showed ABC Fabricators how switching to a Level Funded plan could save them over 18% compared to renewing the existing corporate option. The broker explained how being "Level-Funded" meant taking on slightly more risk as an employer to have more control over plan design and unlock potential surpluses. Because Level Funding allowed us to price their specific risks as a small shop with relatively young, healthy employees, we could provide a customizable program. Their broker guided them through the self-funded model, emphasizing it wasn't as scary as it sounds, since they would have stop loss insurance backing them up. The broker told them to think of it like a warranty on a car—you're protected from the catastrophic, but you take ownership of routine expenses and maintenance.

ABC was hesitant to move off the fully insured plan. They worried about risk and unexpected costs. But after showing various projections based on the shop's sterling claims history, the broker managed to convince them to give Level Funding a shot.

The first year worked reasonably well, although they did end the year with a small deficit due to a few large claims. But in years two and beyond, ABC Fabricators had remarkably positive loss ratios. By year three we were already seeing surpluses accumulating, and by year four I was able to send a surplus check for just over $14,000, or about $450 per covered member, back to the company.

Beyond the refund, the stabilization of their annual premiums allowed ABC Fabricators to direct more money toward hiring an innovative young welding tech. As the guy who manages their company health plan, I can't take all the credit of course. But that surplus check delivered a win for my team. Not only had we provided major upfront savings, but we'd backed it up by returning money directly to the client.

The refund built immense trust and goodwill—clearly, we had lived up to our promises. So, what made this possible when ABC's previous brokers had failed to deliver anything other than rising rates? By taking time to understand a small shop's risk profile, we could use Level Funding to offer a customized solution catered to their unique pool of talent. Price and coverage finally aligned with their firm's needs.

By carving out niche expertise around Level Funding, I've successfully differentiated myself from competitors in an industry crowded with generic "one size fits none" plan offerings. Savvy agents can break free from the constraints of the traditional model by putting small groups at the center of their own plans.

The difference between short and long-term thinking came up in another situation I faced. One of my clients was being courted aggressively by a major health insurer promising first-year rates significantly below their existing premiums. On the surface, it looked very attractive —who doesn't like saving buckets of cash upfront? But as we reviewed the two plans' coverage details side-by-side, critical differences emerged beneath the flashy premium rates. The big-name carrier was cutting costs by shrinking networks and reducing options.

I presented the business owner with a complete picture of how these changes would affect his employees. Although I couldn't match the basement-level premiums, I demonstrated superior value via the specialized pharmacy access one employee desperately needed. I highlighted our rock-solid renewal consistency over the past decade versus the other insurer's pattern of losing customers after the first year. It came down to short-term savings vs long-term stability.

By walking through projected costs over a 5-year span, I showed this client that staying with me was smarter than falling for a short-term rate tease. The strength of our relationship provided the trust needed to rebuff an aggressive poaching attempt from a brand-name competitor promising a quick discount.

But if Level Funding is a great option for many companies, why is it so unheard of? Level Funding upends traditional broker commissions, so most established agents are incentivized to suppress knowledge of this offering. They shy away from rocking the boat. And besides, if you were comfortably making $200,000+ per year, how motivated would you be to change your ways?

This is not to say there is no reward for the noble agent. Thankfully, new agents have a prime opportunity to gain an edge by embracing differentiated solutions. You can be a game-changing pioneer simply by taking time to understand the mechanics of Level Funding. You don't have to compete head-to-head with Spreadsheeters, presenting generic corporate rate sheets like everyone else. By taking a consultative approach to craft tailored plans reflecting each company's unique vision and objectives, you set both yourself and your clients up for lucrative, lasting success.

THE BIG MONEY CORPORATE PROBLEM

"The problem with a big system is that it loses its humanity."
— Unknown

To succeed in the health insurance business it helps to understand how the system works, why it is so inefficient, and how the burdens fall disproportionately on small businesses. The path that led to employer-sponsored health insurance plans today shows how a series of decisions originally intended to provide affordable care became convoluted. For motivated new agents, tracing this evolution is crucial for recognizing the opportunities in today's market.

Many Americans take it for granted that health insurance is covered by employers, but this system is actually quite rare for most of the world. In fact, it was an arbitrary tax loophole that first set the United States off on the course of Big Healthcare. It goes back to the building of the country's railroads.

In the late 19th century, while thousands of men all over the country were laying down railroad tracks, the railroad companies were looking for ways to retain these workers. The companies needed thousands of miles of new track each year. However, the job was not without its risks, and workers were often prone to injury.

Railroad companies were among the first to offer medical benefits for injuries sustained on the job. They needed ways to attract and retain workers. Providing health coverage through company-appointed physicians caught on as an innovative strategy for employee recruitment and retention. This model provided the genesis for our current system of employer-sponsored health coverage.

As railroad companies contracted with hospitals along their routes to care for sick or injured workers, a precedent emerged for corporate health plans that would become more formalized by the turn of the 20th century. With industry consolidation, larger railroads began to use their expansive networks as leverage in negotiations with medical providers. The increasing size and risk-pooling capacity of these early plans allowed enhanced value through economies of scale and improved the predictability of expenses.

While initially limited in scope, the availability of company-subsidized healthcare steadily expanded for certain industries over the ensuing decades. Still, on the eve of World War II, only about 20 million working Americans had any health insurance at all. The vast majority paid cash for care, often negotiating costs directly with local doctors.

Then, during World War II, conflicting wartime policies created a chain reaction that accelerated employer-sponsored insurance as the backbone of medical access in America. First, given massive public spending on military production, President Franklin D. Roosevelt instituted wage caps to "prevent" inflation. To circumvent these limits when competing for talent, companies like Kaiser Shipbuilding (which existed simultaneously with Kaiser Permanente) leveraged fringe benefits like health insurance that were exempt from wage controls. This exemption for benefits gave employers immense latitude to use rich health plans for attracting talent despite capped salaries.

Simultaneously, FDR raised income taxes to extremely high levels to help finance the ballooning war effort. Top brackets could exceed 90-percent. These tax hikes made tax-free fringe benefits even more appealing. With wages capped and income taxes maxed out, tax-exempt compensation like employer-sponsored health insurance was the best way to attract, retain, and better compensate workers.

Within a decade, employer-sponsored health insurance transformed from a rare perk to the predominant form of healthcare coverage for working Americans. And it was this rapid shift that laid the foundation for the U.S. healthcare system's eventual coupling to employers.

Initially, the small scale of local hospital networks and direct risk relationships between regional businesses and medical providers exerted downward pressures on prices. But as health systems consolidated and employment grew less static, the connectivity tying employee wellbeing to nearby community health facilities began to dissipate. Care delivery went from neighborhood doctors billing reasonable rates to large bureaucracies managing faceless patients.

While economies of scale lowered some health plan administrative costs, it also weakened transparency and inflated prices as expansive networks consumed independent providers. The accountability linking healthcare utilization decisions to directly visible neighborhood impacts eroded. The ability for small groups to influence local care ecosystems declined markedly amidst national corporatization.

The outcome is today's landscape where mammoth hospital chains and gargantuan insurers collide over epic medical bills. Smaller employers face minimal leverage to impact cost decisions dictated from afar. Their diminished market share renders stability elusive despite reform efforts. Until both care delivery and insurance supervision rescale toward agile responsiveness, pricing headaches will likely continue without true market corrections arising from local economic pressures.

While these changes ameliorated some healthcare access problems in the short run, the entwining of insurance and employment also created dynamics leading to today's cost and complexity crises. As health plans became primary drivers of talent recruitment, coverage improved substantially for many employees. This in turn boosted employee utilization of the plans.

At first, costs were manageable since risk pools mostly comprised young, healthy factory workers. Over time, though, as innovative treatments emerged and utilization increased, expenses began to weigh more heavily on corporate budgets. This set up a push and pull between cost containment efforts by executives and pushback against reductions from labor unions. Gradually, a multi-tiered system developed with large companies benefiting from economies of scale, but smaller firms and unions left marginalized.

Understanding this tangled history provides context for modern healthcare debates by illuminating how decisions meant to help workers also sowed seeds of the current system's inefficiencies, which disproportionately impact small businesses today. While employer-sponsored plans improved access for many employees, they also established financial entanglements and incentives misalignments contributing to cost inflation pressures.

Appreciating these complex origins is key for innovating smarter solutions to help small companies struggling with rising expenses and waning influence. As emerging innovations like direct primary care and value-based arrangements aim to recover healthcare's lost intimacy through small-scale experimentation, they face relentless countervailing consolidation forces. Nonetheless, resolute visionaries push forward seeking workarounds that thread regulatory needles to spark competition and light fires under lumbering old giants.

Today, we stand at a crossroads as an industry. Do we continue concentrating power in gargantuan bureaucracies that are ballooning into slow-moving monopolies? Or does market redemption arise when nimble actuaries and lucid physicians conspire to restore choice through industry innovation? The years ahead will determine whether corporatized healthcare's supernova implodes toward renewed decentralization, or perpetuates at the cost of billions of dollars to small businesses.

THE VALUE AND COSTS OF AMERICAN HEALTHCARE INNOVATION

"Ideal systems are big enough to be efficient, but small enough to be human."
— *Unknown*

America's healthcare system stands unrivaled globally for pioneering cutting-edge treatments and breakthrough technologies. Pharmaceutical firms invest over $90 billion annually in the development of innovative therapies that raise standards worldwide. Top academic hospitals conduct extensive research unearthing revolutionary interventions that overcome once incurable illnesses. This relentless innovation engine fuels discoveries that benefit all humanity.

However, critics argue that America's leadership in subsidizing medical advancements for the globe comes at a staggering domestic cost. As utilization surges for sophisticated diagnostics, gene therapies, and surgical robots, health spending threatens to cause financial headwinds for families and strain budgets beyond sustainable limits absent proportional economic expansion.

I encountered this dichotomy between innovation benefits and affordability challenges firsthand during a chance airport encounter. While waiting to board a flight from Houston to Calgary, I struck up conversation with the woman seated next to me. She was in an arm sling.

"Going home for surgery?" I asked.

"No," she said, "I just got the surgery. Now I'm going back home."

"Wait," I said, puzzled. "Don't you Canadians have free healthcare? Why would you fly all the way to Houston for surgery?"

"I'm 60 years old," she said. "I could have got my shoulder operated on in Canada for free, but I would have had to wait nine months. At my age, I don't know how many years I have left, so I'm not going to sit around in pain waiting. Instead, it was worth it to me to cough up $50,000 American dollars to fly down here and get my operation immediately, and from a world-class specialist no less."

This vignette highlights how America's system essentially subsidizes global medical advancement through higher costs concentrated in one nation. Insured Americans fund phenomenal care through rising premiums. Yet, even for Americans, accessing cutting-edge treatments increasingly causes financial trauma, pitting health against viability.

Nowhere do innovation tensions manifest more severely than with gene and cell therapies. These treatments can cure formerly life-shortening illnesses, but at costs exceeding $8 million per course. While these breakthroughs spark jubilation for desperate families, pricing shockwaves threaten hospitals that are currently aiding millions more through traditional care.

As unprecedented cures emerge, a critical question arises: who should determine the financial responsibilities associated with these treatments? Consider childhood leukemia, an emotionally and financially devastating ordeal for most families. Remarkably, gene therapy has emerged as a game-changer, with a single infusion curing 97% of a specific type of leukemia. However, with prices exceeding $475,000 per dose, how should families and hospitals budget for these life-saving treatments that often surpass middle-class affordability? What happens when responsible parents face the heartbreaking choice of losing their homes to secure their child's restored future?

Of course, even adamant capitalists blanch at business models denying proven lifesaving interventions solely due to customers' income levels. For now, pharmaceutical firms force hospitals to absorb six-figure therapy costs through higher general patient charges. But as 100+ gene and cell treatments near federal approval, current funding models cannot sustain ballooning expenses concentrated within one nation.

While urgent cases present gut-wrenching appeals, medical economists note roughly half of healthcare spending finances routine cases more amenable to oversight. As transparency improves around actual research investments influencing policy historically, future regulations will likely pressure health corporations via pricing caps closer to international norms. This shift may provide relief for government budgets, but risks jeopardizing America's preeminence in developing future cures without alternative funding streams.

Under America's capitalistic approach, the potential for outsized industry profits incentivizes high-risk investments into bio-pharma R&D. Attempts to socialize medicine without preserving cash flows supporting innovation risk the unintended consequence of stifling new discoveries. However, unfettered pricing power currently threatens to bankrupt families seeking last-hope treatments unaffordable to nearly all households. Where should the ethical lines be drawn? How can America uphold its standard of healthcare innovation while controlling costs concentrated domestically? This is not a new challenge. In fact, it is as old as the enlightenment. How do we balance the wealth of nations with the theory of moral sentiments?

Even the most reasonable people tend to disagree on solutions, with proposals spanning from single-payer systems capping profits to tech-centric approaches aiming to unlock free-market efficiencies, reducing frictions and added costs. However, evidence suggests feasible answers integrate selected centralized and decentralized elements. Just as modern societies require shared infrastructure investments beyond most individuals' capacity, modern medical breakthroughs rely on entities with capital depths that surpass the combined wealth of citizens and communities. Nonetheless, swelling resentment against detached bureaucratic pricing models threatens urgent calls for radical systemic reforms.

With patients squeezed by costs and alienated from decision-making bodies, restoring public trust demands responsive solutions. As consumers shoulder outsized financial burdens, appeals heighten for recalibrating charges beyond one nation's limits. In the years ahead, sustainable innovation requires health corporations to embrace pricing within profitability ranges deemed fair through a socio-economic lens.

As healthcare captures nearly 20% of America's GDP—heading toward a quarter in the next decade—debates around appropriate cost controls and access are expected to intensify. The ethical challenge ahead goes beyond political rhetoric. It requires collective soul searching around the moral obligations of a society to uplift the civilization as a whole versus protecting vulnerable community members locally at a disproportionate cost to the whole.

There may not be a perfect solution, but there is certainly a better one than the current system we have today. It may be uncomfortable, but it is a better society that has questions you can't answer than answers you can't question.

THE PHILOSOPHY OF INSURANCE: BALANCING RISK AND REWARD

"Show me the incentive and I'll show you the outcome."
— *Charlie Munger*

I once asked a room full of fresh, young brokers, "What is insurance?" Their response: crickets. Blank stares. It was as if to say, *Who cares,*

Tom! We sell it and people buy it! But to ensure that what we are selling is actually valuable, it's worth it to understand what the heck it is.

Insurance is a fascinating concept that has shaped the course of human history in ways that people often overlook. At its core, insurance manages risk and distributes the cost of unexpected events across a larger pool of people. It harnesses the power of collective action to protect individuals and society as a whole from the devastating impact of catastrophic losses.

But insurance is not just a financial tool. It's also a philosophical and moral construct that reflects human beliefs about responsibility and the role of government in our lives. By studying the history and evolution of insurance, we can gain valuable insights into the human condition and the challenges we face in building a more just and equitable world.

So, what exactly is insurance? In its most basic form, insurance pools risk among a group of people who all face a similar potential loss. The idea is that by spreading the cost of that potential loss across a larger group, it minimizes the impact on any one individual. People often describe insurance as "the lucky many paying for the unlucky few," because the premiums paid by the majority of policyholders who don't experience a loss compensate the minority who do.

At a deeper level, we can see insurance as a form of social solidarity —a way of expressing our shared responsibility to protect and care for one another in times of need. It's a system that embodies a collective social agreement that aims to balance the interests of all parties involved. Insurance enables action and enterprise by providing a semblance of protection against misfortune through collective means.

This idea of collective responsibility has deep roots in human history, predating the establishment of formal insurance systems. One of the earliest examples of modern insurance dates back to the 14th century, when merchants in the Italian city-states began pooling their resources to protect against the risk of shipwrecks and piracy. By paying into a common fund, merchants spread the cost of potential losses across the entire group, rather than bearing the full burden themselves.

Collective risk pooling has existed since the establishment of states, not just from the 14th century. The 14th-century example is significant because it marks the first time this was done using Type-3 money. Additionally, this early form of marine insurance led to the development of industry standards and regulations, such as marine law. When the individual had skin in the game, more attention was paid to the systems dictating how their money was used.

Similarly, the Great Fire of London in the 17th century prompted the creation of the first fire insurance companies. These companies provided protection against the risk of property damage in exchange for regular premiums. Insurance companies, through their underwriting practices, created economic incentives for the adoption of safer practices and technologies.

The growth of insurance in the modern era is closely linked to the rise of capitalism and the industrialization of society. As people and businesses become more interconnected and interdependent, the need for mechanisms to manage and mitigate risk increases. Today, insurance is a massive global industry, with trillions of dollars in premiums paid annually to protect against various risks, including car accidents, natural disasters, medical emergencies, and cyberattacks.

Throughout history, insurance has also played a role in supporting social welfare and protecting vulnerable populations. The establishment of social insurance programs like workers' compensation, unemployment insurance, and Social Security in the early 1900s created a basic safety net for millions of Americans during tough times.

However, it's important to note that these programs have faced ongoing actuarial challenges and debates. The shift from true insurance models to more politically-driven systems, often relying on Type-4 money, has raised questions about their long-term sustainability. As our political leaders have often treated these programs as the "third rail" of American politics, reforms have been difficult, leading to hidden reductions in benefits and increased reliance on debt and monetary expansion.

In recent years, the rise of micro-insurance, Microfinance, and micro-banking programs in developing countries has helped extend insurance benefits to millions of low-income households around the world. These market-driven innovations—made possible by the incentives of Type-3 money—offer small-scale policies to protect against risks like illness, injury, and crop failure. They have had a significant impact on reducing poverty and promoting economic development, while also increasing the value of labor through specialization.

As we look to the future, insurance will continue to shape the course of human history. With the rise of new technologies and the increasing complexity of global challenges, the potential for innovation in risk management is greater than ever before. At the same time, we must grapple with profound questions about how we choose to manage and distribute risk in a way that promotes the common good.

The balance between individual responsibility and collective protection lies at the heart of the philosophy of insurance. On one level, we are all responsible for our own actions and the risks we choose to take. But as members of a society, we also have a shared obligation to look out for one another and to create systems that provide a basic level of security for all.

Finding the right balance between these competing imperatives is no easy task. It requires us to think deeply about the nature of risk, the limits of individual autonomy, and the role of collective action in promoting the greater good. It demands that we confront difficult questions about fairness, equality, and the distribution of resources in an increasingly complex and interconnected world.

The effectiveness of insurance and risk-pooling systems is closely tied to the level of social trust within a society. In communities with high levels of trust and voluntary cooperation, collective action to manage risk can be incredibly efficient and effective. I recently had a striking personal experience that illustrates this point.

A friend of mine, who is Amish, woke up one morning to find that his shop burned down to the ground, taking with it all the inventory he spent years building. When I offered to help, he simply asked for assistance in printing flyers for a reopening the following week. The collective action taken by the Amish community, through entirely voluntary exchange, astounded me with its speed and effectiveness. It boggles my mind to see how quickly action is taken and completed when systems have high social trust.

This level of trust is, in many ways, the true wealth of a nation. As the saying goes, "Where there is no law, there is no bread." But law is only enforceable through the consent of the governed, and it is the trust of the people in society that enables there to be bread. The higher the trust, the wealthier the nation.

Agreeing on the law is an ongoing struggle. I recently reached out to some industry veterans and asked them the same question I asked the young brokers at the start of this section: "What is insurance?" Surprisingly, even these seasoned professionals struggled to provide a concise answer. It's striking that those who have spent decades in the insurance industry still grapple with articulating a clear definition of what insurance is and why it matters. This difficulty points to the inherent complexity that insurance seeks to address.

By examining the history and philosophy of insurance, we can gain valuable insights into the human condition and imagine new forms of collective action that can help us navigate an uncertain future. The decisions we make about risk management in the coming years will have a significant impact on the world we leave for future generations.

SHIFTS IN HEALTHCARE PAYMENT MODELS

"People see the world not as it is, but from what they understand."
— Unknown

The evolution of healthcare financing in America reflects an ongoing cycle of cost escalations across models. This pattern has triggered various reforms to curb spending. However, as savings from new approaches diminish over time, systemic imbalances bring about the need for new corrections. Understanding this cycle provides perspective on why achieving optimal balance across affordability, patient choice, customized care, and medical innovation remains an elusive quest.

In the early 20th century, basic indemnity health plans predominated coverage, wherein patients paid out-of-pocket for medical services then filed claims for reimbursement by insurers. This straightforward model afforded freedom in choosing providers and treatments. However, due to a lack of coordinated cost oversight, prices grew higher, violating the "brother rule" — if your brother said the same thing to you, would you punch him in the face? If so, it violates the brother rule.

For example, "Hey bro! I think there's a problem with my oldsmobile. Would you mind taking a look under the hood so I know who to go to for repairs?"

"Sure thing, pal. That'll cost ya $500."

After punching him in the face, he agrees to do it for coffee and lunch instead.

Seeking to constrain runaway inflation under indemnity plans, Health Maintenance Organizations (HMOs) emerged in the 1970s as prepaid coverage plans built around tightly managed networks under prospective budgeting models. HMOs emphasized prevention and efficient case management by using primary care gatekeeping and restricted specialist referrals. At first, this structure slowed cost growth. However, compared to indemnity arrangements, the limited choices of HMOs eventually provoked customer dissatisfaction, because the incentives encouraged bad-brother actions.

Preferred Provider Organizations (PPOs) developed in the 1980s and 90s, partly in response to mounting frustrations over narrow HMO networks. PPOs negotiate discounted service fees with contracted physician groups and hospitals in exchange for patient volume. Participants retain options to access out-of-network providers, typically at higher out-of-pocket costs. Relative to restrictive HMOs, PPOs were better at balancing open access considerations with costs. This hybrid model fueled small group plan adoption throughout the 1990s.

However, two key developments over recent decades have challenged PPOs' ability to constrain expense growth. First, consolidating hospital groups gained disproportionate market share relative to large insurers, thus undermining discounts. Second, expanded PPO networks introduced redundancies into consumer care. Multiplied access points for users sounds great until they start bouncing around between doctors and needing tests redone lacking shared records. This compounded costs, again violating the brother rule.

Seeking stronger cost controls given eroding PPO savings, Reference Based Pricing (RBP) models recently emerged, inspired by earlier indemnity models but adding defined pricing data parameters. Under RBP, payers establish claims reimbursement ceilings based on Medicare rates for procedures rather than relying solely on hospital charges. This approach leverages benchmarking to limit pricing variability exploitation. If costs exceed predefined limits, plan participants cover additional charges via supplemental plans or cash.

Conceptually, RBP introduces greater claims clarity relative to PPOs. However, some hospitals reject rules that cap viable charges below desired ranges. This poses a risk of access barriers for patients if the participation of hospitals remains uncertain. In other words, hospitals don't have to agree to pricing models, even if the ceiling is 10x the rates for Medicare. For some hospitals, their preferred ceilings can be as high as 3,000x the rates for Medicare! That's like your brother charging six figures for an oil change. Yeah, he's getting punched in the face. Naturally, billing disputes arise when charges exceed reference rates, and care providers still expect full collection from individual patients.

In response to criticism, many insurers now pursue transitional options, like layered RBP contracts, that minimize client balance billing exposures while still advancing reference pricing mechanisms. These arrangements aim to bring pricing transparency in light of current hospital protections. Providers of layered RBP contracts, aware of the risks of shifting delivery cost burdens to individuals, also spend more time instilling balance billing protections into the agreements. They are aware that individuals seeking health care are poorly positioned to shoulder financial liabilities based on decisions made by institutions, especially when the institutions favor profitability over consumer-centric caretaking, a clear violation of the brother rule.

There is another layer to the evolving healthcare models, and that is the one that pits larger insurance providers against the smaller ones. While large insurers focus resources on bigger accounts, smaller groups are left with a painful decision. Do they focus their limited resources on competing with the big boys using proven models? Or do they risk innovating new models?

Expanding personalized care options may offer opportunities to redesign systems in local communities. As direct primary care models shift basic healthcare services to a more accessible level, market dynamics could disrupt traditional healthcare structures. Smaller practices, leveraging simple and transparent pricing, circumvent conventional insurance models while prioritizing doctor-patient relationships. This shift prompts a reevaluation of healthcare's scope and structure, moving away from systems characterized by alternating cycles of consolidation and cost escalation driven by excessive provider leverage.

From early indemnity, through modern HMO and PPO variants and contemporary RBP experiments, we see an endless sequence of market corrections. When insurance costs get out of hand, new models steer costs back down. Indeed, change itself remains healthcare's sole, steadfast certainty.

The history of American healthcare financing reveals the risks of searching for singular panaceas while obscuring the faces of supported patients behind policies. Evidence increasingly suggests progress arises from empowering local agents instead of central planning authorities. Doing so not only localizes social contracts, but secures flexibility for future innovators to take clinical risks on behalf of community health.

CHALLENGES FACED BY SMALL GROUPS UNDER CURRENT SYSTEMS

"When small, it is best to be nimble."
— Unknown

Small businesses seeking to provide health coverage for their employees face disproportionate difficulties while competing within frameworks that favor large corporations. The complex regulations governing self-funded arrangements often lock out smaller groups from implementing customized plans. But with a strategic approach and careful underwriting, it is possible to design plans that pair flexibility with the potential for surplus funds.

We must start by noting the role of the Affordable Care Act (ACA). The ACA imposes minimum loss ratio requirements upon insurers, stipulating that no more than 20 percent of all premium dollars may go toward administrative expenses and profit. This aims to ensure that the majority of monies collected are directed into actual care delivery. For small businesses, though, broker commissions, plan administration fees, and stop-loss premiums can reasonably exceed thresholds. This triggers rebates owed to policyholders.

The main problem here is that regulations lump small business plans together with mega corporations. Without lobbying leverage, small company plans get categorized similarly to national mega-insurers boasting billion-dollar reserve assets. This is despite the fact that reasonable overhead for a startup is drastically different from that of bigger competitors, violating the brother rule.

It's like saying, "Hey bro! Can you watch my dog for the weekend?"

And he says, "Sure thing, pal. I just need a $5,000 emergency fund in case something happens."

After a punch in the face he agrees to watch your dog free of charge, and if something *does* happen then he'll cover the cost and you'll reimburse him when you get back.

The ACA's employer mandate imposes compliance burdens that disproportionately affect small business owners. SMB owners often lack specialized HR expertise. Consequently, determining workforce categories qualifying for health benefits as per complex eligibility definitions, tracking hours accurately, compiling extensive reporting, and avoiding the potential for severe IRS penalties all require significant time investments or expensive vendor partnerships. These requirements erode the very cost savings that self-funding intends to create for these groups.

Anecdotally, many states also establish loss corridor requirements that appear intentionally structured to discourage self-funded health plans among smaller employers. For example, Alaska regulations contain a minimum $4,000 aggregate funding per life for groups with less than 50 employees. Deductible minimums per person then disappear for larger groups above 50 covered lives. Designing affordable plans given such high mandatory floor costs often proves unworkable for modest-sized employee populations. Yet, conveniently, once crossing arbitrary group size thresholds, the mathematical barriers to self-funding options drop significantly.

In other jurisdictions across the nation, constraints with similar effects can be observed. In Colorado, mandated deductibles for self-funded arrangements exhibit a peculiar trend: as the group size exceeds 50 workers, the deductibles decrease, resulting in thousands more in required plan spending for smaller employer budgets.

One need not endorse shadowy conspiracy theories to reasonably question apparent patterns within certain state regulations—and by extension federal laws—whereby calculated barriers ration access to self-funding for primarily larger entities with the means to surmount the erected obstacles. These overwhelming structural disadvantages partially explain the extremely low market penetration of self-funded arrangements among small employers today. Put simply, when rules make the minimum number of people needed to be profitable too high, smaller groups don't have many options.

Small businesses trying to offer employee health coverage face substantial obstacles under the predominant corporate insurance models. Lacking extensive risk pools for predictable actuarial projections, smaller groups have difficulty securing affordable policies that align with their budgets and aspirations. This places family enterprises and younger startups at inherent disadvantages relative to more established competitors with thousands of lives under management.

Understanding the regulatory hurdles ingrained in current systems is crucial for charting pathways that enable small business owners to take control of health plans in ways that benefit their workforce and communities. With some resolution around key areas of debate, small businesses could pool collective interests to restructure systems. If software launching out of dorm rooms upended entire industries, then innovative medical groups partnering with local small business leaders also contain transformational seeds. They only need a minimal garden bed of policy to regrow community caretaking countrywide.

As healthcare costs continue to rise faster than broader economic inflation, smaller employers face ever-steeper climbs. Unlike large corporations wielding immense negotiating leverage, modestly sized companies lack the buying power to significantly influence insurer rate decisions. This leaves small businesses perennially vulnerable to soaring premiums and restrictive plan adjustments that weaken coverage over time, absent recourse.

When overall premiums spike due to exceptional utilization patterns by a few mammoth accounts, smaller groups disproportionately absorb rate escalations passed down without consultation. Many stop loss captives—devised by associations that represent larger employers—structurally exclude smaller players through the erection of costly financial and administrative participation hurdles. This cements lower-middle-market marginalization. In other words, resource concentration exacerbates wealth divides.

Existing corporate health insurance structures often marginalize small groups due to economies of scale, but this does create an opportunity for an approach tailored to small businesses, an approach like Level Funding. Extensive research reveals nearly 90% of covered U.S. workers are in smaller settings of under 100 employees. This vast yet fragmented constituency deserves an approach to match that of their size. Insurer innovators engaging the under-100 space can uncover urgent, unmet needs. All they must do is challenge the assumption that sheer corporate bulk always drives the best outcome.

Underwriting freedom is the root of insurer accountability to any group, regardless of size. Still, legacy regulations handicap smaller risk pools, preventing carriers from structuring plans responsive to distinctive challenges. Inflexible models demanding conformity with one-dimensional benchmarks disproportionately hurt specialized customers. For example, state regulations can often cap permissible risk contributions for groups of 5 to 100 covered workers below sustainability levels, absent credible claims history or multi-year commitments securing financial viability for plan sponsors.

Workplaces need not accept false dichotomies that force binary choices between corporate scale and humane flexibility. Ethical visionaries are developing solutions that optimize care quality through bottom-up innovation, not just top-down austerity. My team routinely develops cost-effective offerings tightly aligned with nuanced organizational aspirations. And we do this for customers sized 5 to 100 covered workers.

We win trust through accountability. Our national stop-loss providers remark on the incredible precision we have in predicting risk across books filled exclusively with companies under 50. And every year, claim expenses match initial loss projections within a few percentage points on average, generally shocking executives accustomed to the volatility of small groups. Confidence grows further when we deliver surplus checks to our clients, transforming their skepticism into enthusiasm. Business owners love it when self-directed plans can return tangible value, especially when compared to incumbent structures that allow waste and restrict reinvestment, violating the brother rule.

It's like saying, "Hey bro! Thanks for helping replace my windows. That was a huge help. Here's $1,000."

And then one week later your brother is at your door, saying, "Hey pal, I lost a bet and now I need some money. Can you spot me rent this month?"

In essence, existing systems disproportionately centralize profits and decision-making power around larger entities better positioned to dictate terms by exploiting economies of scale. Smaller groups suffer limited choices, inconsistent pricing, and minimal influence over plan adjustments that could better serve their needs. Plans like Level Funding can serve an urgent need by providing flexible plans to small businesses that otherwise have to pay for expensive plans that don't fit their needs.

INNOVATIVE APPROACHES WITHIN CONSTRAINED SYSTEMS

"Creativity requires the courage to let go of certainties."
— Erich Fromm

Despite the constraints presented by existing payment structures and regulations, daring approaches—such as Direct Primary Care (DPC) models, telemedicine, and innovative insurance strategies—exemplify the fertile ground for building a remarkable career in health insurance. By understanding and leveraging Level Funding tailored to the under-100 employee market, insurance agents can help small businesses navigate the inefficiencies of traditional insurance frameworks and find economic viability.

Direct Primary Care (DPC) is an innovative model that significantly reimagines primary care delivery. It operates under transparent, low-cost monthly fees, instead of perplexing insurance billing for routine visits and basic services. This model allows doctors and nurse practitioners to have patient panels capped around 500-1000 patients —far fewer than the 2500-plus required by many corporate providers under typical reimbursement rules. Such a sizable financial difference is precisely where the role of Level Funding comes into play. By offering predictably priced insurance plans that reimburse for health spending up to a certain level, small companies can enjoy the benefits of a more personalized health service without the risk of unpredictable costs.

This dramatic reduction in caseload translates into longer appointment times, strengthened patient-provider relationships, and less time wasted on insurance paperwork. Many small businesses are choosing to pair DPC with wraparound insurance plans using reference-based pricing to cover additional costs involved in hospitalizations and preventive care beyond primary services. With monthly fees ranging between $50-150 per employee, employers can offer the benefits of regular, on-site, or nearby primary care, which often includes extended weekday and weekend hours—factors that influence employee recruitment and retention while potentially reducing costs.

Agents can position DPC as an innovative strategy to provide wellness benefits that align with modern talent demands, particularly appealing to startups and smaller businesses thriving in the digital economy. Even as traditional carriers may resist change, small businesses can see the advantage in consumer-centric care models that better align with their personnel needs. This readiness for innovation creates fresh opportunities for brokers seeking competitive advantages.

Telemedicine is another dynamic service rapidly gaining popularity. Virtual health access through phone apps or video chat sessions offers incredible convenience for addressing common health issues like sore throats or dermatological concerns. Employers appreciate the round-the-clock availability, as telehealth extends care options beyond typical business hours at a fraction of the cost. The significant uptick in telehealth utilization during the COVID-19 pandemic's lockdowns has fueled lasting consumer adoption, shifting it from a niche service for early tech adopters to a mainstream expectation.

For agents, incorporating telemedicine into benefits packages is becoming easier and more cost-effective, with supplementary features starting at roughly $5 per employee per month. Offering telehealth services can reduce long-term insurance costs by addressing minor conditions that would otherwise escalate to more expensive urgent care or emergency room visits. Some forward-thinking brokers are even including basic telemedicine access as a free-added value, differentiating their offerings when competing for new business contracts.

The key to successfully navigating these constrained systems lies in identifying the opportunities that exist within their limitations. Innovative solutions like DPC and telehealth are employing technology to meet evolving consumer expectations. Agents willing to test unorthodox ideas can sidestep traditional barriers, reframing care delivery models to prioritize flexibility and convenience.

Brokers must maintain an experimental mindset as additional innovations like artificial intelligence in clinical decision-making and genomic testing emerge. This emerging technology has the potential to offer enhanced efficiencies or care differentiation. Agile brokers continuously scout the landscape for next-generation solutions that service niche markets overlooked by larger players married to outmoded revenue models and conventional wisdom.

Healthcare's complex legacy systems, fraught with misaligned incentives and concentrated power, tend to obstruct change-makers who threaten the status quo. Large incumbents often protect their privileged positions, thereby curbing consumer choice. Nevertheless, resourceful visionaries are finding ways to navigate these obstacles, reimagining community health relationships beyond the mere transactional delivery of care. These brave individuals are fulfilling a broader social contract that secures the flexibility needed for future innovators willing to take the calculated risk to perfect and scale creative models that could transform the healthcare industry.

As we move forward, traditional healthcare norms will likely face an unprecedented challenge as disruptive concepts shift control and financing toward more consumer-centric paradigms. Successful agents will recognize the transitional opportunities that arise from this transformational crisis by advising those who are crafting more principled and sustainable systems. This pivotal moment in healthcare calls for a reinvigoration of the industry's essence—redesigning insurance and clinical models around community accountability, affordability, and choice, in line with the brother rule. It is indeed time for a new path forward...A path that insurance agents can chart by understanding and advocating for innovative solutions like Level Funding for their clients.

But the journey will not be easy. Entrenched interests and outdated regulations will undoubtedly push back against any efforts to disrupt the status quo. Brokers who choose to be pioneers in this space will need to be resilient, adaptable, and unwavering in their commitment to their clients' best interests.

Agents must serve as educators, guiding employers and employees alike in comprehending the complexities of these novel models and their potential advantages. They must act as advocates, championing policies that create a level playing field for small businesses and empower them to innovate. Additionally, they should be collaborative partners, working closely with clients to create and execute tailored plans that align with their specific requirements.

Most importantly, they will need to be guided by a strong moral compass, one that always puts the well-being of patients and the sustainability of the healthcare system ahead of short-term profits. This means adhering to the brother rule, treating clients with the same respect and fairness they would expect from a trusted sibling. It means being transparent about the risks and rewards of different options, and never pushing a solution just because it benefits the bottom line.

In the end, the brokers who will thrive in this new era of healthcare will be those who are willing to think outside the box, challenge conventional wisdom, and put in the hard work required to drive meaningful change. They will be the ones who recognize that the ultimate measure of success is not just in the numbers, but in the lives they touch and the communities they strengthen.

The Level-Funded revolution is not just about transforming how we pay for healthcare. It's about reimagining what healthcare can and should be, and empowering those on the front lines to make that vision a reality. It's about restoring humanity to a system that has become too big, too complex, and too impersonal. And it's about giving small businesses and their employees the tools they need to take control of their health and their future.

LEVEL FUNDING 101: KEY TERMS AND CONCEPTS

Since you are a fully certified insurance broker, I trust you know your stuff. If you're newly minted, then you probably still have your head crammed full of insurance terms and definitions. However, Level Funding has a way of adding a little twist to frequently used terms in the industry. For that reason, I'm providing a list of key terms and phrases you can expect to see in this book.

It is worth noting that many terms and phrases in health insurance are used synonymously. I catch myself switching between two different phrases meaning the same thing all the time. If you want a career in this industry, I recommend you get used to this reality.

Please take a minute to review the following terms and phrases.* That way we can be on the same page moving forward. Literally.

This is a general guide to the market, and some definitions may be different with different operators.

1. **Aggregate Stop-Loss / ASL / Agg / Aggregate Stop-Loss Insurance:** This is what provides a maximum qualified claim liability for the entire group.

2. **Aggregating Specific Corridor / Aggregating Specific Deductible / Aggregating Spec:** This contract provision is often offered in TPA (third party administrator) arrangements. It is an extra form of risk to the employer on large claimant(s) exceeding the Individual Stop Loss (see below), which reduces premiums on their quote. The aggregating specific increases the likelihood of the employer hitting their aggregate claim liability, and reduces the risk on the individual stop loss policy.

3. **Claims Corridor / Corridor Factor / Risk Corridor / Attachment Corridor / Attachment Percentage:** The area that represents the risk corridor above expected claims. For Level Funding products, this corridor is typically 10

percent except where state mandates require higher. For Graded Funding (see MAF below), this corridor is typically 20 or 25 percent.

4. **Claims Funding (Level Funding) / Claim Liability / Maximum Claim Exposure / Monthly Claims Funding (MCF) / Maximum Claims Liability**: Typically expressed on a per-month basis, the claims funding is used to define the amount which the client will be paying for claims in a plan year. At year-end this number is compared against total paid claims for the year to determine if there is a surplus available.

5. **Contract Period / Incurred Period / Paid Period / Coverage Period / Policy Period:** The time covered under a contract designating when a claim is incurred and when the claim must be paid to qualify for reimbursement.

6. **Contract Type [12/12, 15/12, 12/15, 12/18, 12/24] Paid:** This refers to contracts typically seen in self-funded arrangements that are offered through TPAs (third party administrators) along with a reinsurer. The first number refers to the "Incurral Period" and the second number refers to the "Paid Period". For example, a 12/12 contract covers all qualifying claims that are both incurred and paid within the 12-month contract period, while a 12/18 contract covers all qualifying claims incurred within the 12-month contract period and paid within 18 months of the contract start date.

7. **Credibility:** When underwriting claims experience (either for a prospect or for a renewal), the client's claims experience is assigned a 'credibility' factor (see Experience Underwriting below). This loosely translates to a "predictability factor" based on size of the group, timeframe of the experience period (mature or immature

experience period), pooling level, and expected large claims. The larger the group, the higher their credibility.

8. **Eligibility Roster / Census Report / List of Covered Members / Coverage Report:** This is the employee listing usually provided by the insurer, and in some cases is available through the insurer's proprietary online systems.

9. **Expected Claims / Claims Expected:** The dollar amount of claims anticipated to be paid based on a plan's characteristics.

10. **Experience Underwriting / Credibility Based Underwriting:** This refers to a method of underwriting both at presale and renewal which factors in the client's previous year's claims experience to predict future claim costs.

11. **Fixed Costs / Admin & Insurance / A&I / Fees / Premiums:** These consist of Administration Fees, Commissions (if applicable), the Individual Stop Loss Premium, and the Aggregate Stop Loss Premium. Paid monthly based on enrollment.

12. **IBNR / Incurred but Not Reported or Revealed Claims:** Claims that have been "Incurred But Not Reported". IBNR generally refers to claims that are in the "lag period" that occurs between the date a claim was incurred and the date it will be received for payment.

13. **Lag Report / IBNR Report:** Usually requested for a client's accounting/audit purposes, this report helps them determine an estimated terminal or runout liability, based on lag times seen on the plan during the preceding 12 month period. In other words, it is the average time for claims to be paid.

14. **Laser Exclusion / Adjustment of Stop Loss Coverage for an Individual:** This is an additional form of risk to the employer. For large claimants which may be ongoing,

the stop loss carrier alters the individual stop loss (ISL) coverage for certain claimant(s). For instance, if the client's ISL level is $25,000, an individual with a serious ongoing claim may have their own ISL of $150,000. The difference between the $25,000 and $150,000 may or may not accumulate to the employer's aggregate claim liability, which means they will likely reach or exceed claim liability. Some carriers do not mandate lasers; however, many will consider this upon employer or broker request.

15. **Minimum Attachment / MA:** This is a provision that sets a minimum claim attachment liability in the event the client's enrollment shrinks. This allows the insurer and the client to control costs and risk should the enrollment shrink. It is calculated based upon a percentage of enrollment at the time of renewal (can be 90%, 95%, or 100%). This is typically lower by percentage or not included in Level Funding products.

16. **Monthly Claim Liability / Claim liability / Maximum Claim Exposure / Aggregate Liability / Monthly Attachment Factor (MAF, or Graded Funding) / Monthly Claim Funding (MCF, or Level Funding):** The amount, expressed in dollars per employee (and/or dependent) per month used to define the claim liability for each month. See Attachment Factor and Claims Funding.

17. **Off-Anniversary:** This refers to a date other than the plan's original effective month. For instance a 1/1 client renews each year on 1/1, but if they terminate on 3/1 then they have terminated off-anniversary.

18. **Paid Contract:** A self-funded contract that provides stop loss protection for all claims incurred under the life of the policy paid during the 12 month contract period. Some contracts renew to a paid contract at their first renewal.

19. **Plan Year / Benefit Period:** The 12-month period in which deductible and coinsurance accumulates toward a plan participant's out-of-pocket maximums.

20. **Reinsurance Carrier / Reinsurer:** This is the stop loss carrier's back up on larger claims providing an additional level of pooling behind the scenes and is typically not known to the plan member.

21. **Run-In / A 15/12 Contract:** Claims incurred prior to the first contract year and received after the new effective date. These claims can be paid under a "current year" contract that includes a run-in provision. Some insurers can offer run-in protection on individual stop loss (ISL), but it must be priced for with underwriting. A 15/12 is more protective and therefore has a higher premium, typically.

22. **Run-Out Terminal / Liability Period / Incurred but Not Paid Claims / Run-Off Liability:** The run-out terminal refers to the period of time immediately following termination, during which time all claims incurred prior to the termination date are being paid. Timely claims submission, determination of medical necessity, clarification of issues, and claims processing all contribute to the run-out period. Most contracts provide at least 3 months to 12 months of run-out protection.

23. **Total Costs / Maximum Liability / Fully Funded Rates:** This is the total amount of liability each month consisting of administrative and insurance costs plus monthly claim liability. For Level Funding clients, this represents the total payment they will budget for and pay to the insurer each month.

24. **TPA / Third Party Administrator / Administrator:** Refers to the third party/entity administering a plan (plan documents, paying claims, servicing). May or may not

coordinate with the employer and broker on other 'pieces' such as Rental Network, Disease Management, Wellness Programs, Reinsurance.

Now that we've covered the key terms and concepts related to underwriting Level-Funded plans, let's take a closer look at one of the most critical components of these plans: stop-loss coverage. As a broker, it's essential to have a deep understanding of stop-loss coverage and to effectively communicate this information to your clients.

Stop-loss coverage is a critical component of Level-Funded plans, as it protects the plan from catastrophic claims that could financially devastate the plan's reserves. When explaining stop-loss coverage to clients, it's essential to cover the following key points:

1. **Specific Stop-Loss (SSL) Coverage:** SSL coverage protects the plan from any single claim that exceeds a predetermined threshold. For example, if the SSL deductible is set at $50,000, the stop-loss carrier will reimburse the plan for any amount above that threshold for an individual claim. It's important to note that the stop-loss carrier reimburses the plan, not the employer directly.

2. **Aggregate Stop-Loss (ASL) Coverage:** ASL coverage kicks in when the total claims for the plan exceed a predetermined threshold, known as the aggregate attachment point. This attachment point is typically calculated based on the plan's expected claims, plus a percentage margin (usually 20-25%). If the total claims exceed this threshold, the stop-loss carrier will reimburse the plan for the excess amount.

3. **Lasering:** In some cases, the stop-loss carrier may "laser" an individual with known high-cost claims. This means that the SSL deductible for that specific individual is set at a higher amount than the rest of the group. It's important to

disclose any lasering to the plan sponsor upfront to avoid surprises down the road.

4. **Contract Basis:** Stop-loss coverage can be provided on various contract bases, such as 12/12, 12/15, or 12/24. These numbers represent the months of incurred claims and the months of paid claims covered by the policy. For example, a 12/15 contract covers claims incurred within the 12-month policy period and paid within 3 months of the end of the contract. It's crucial to understand the implications of different contract bases and to explain them clearly to the plan sponsor.

5. **Policyholder:** It's essential to understand that the stop-loss policy should be issued to the plan itself, not the employer. When the policy is issued to the plan, it functions as a reinsurance transaction between two insuring entities. If the policy is issued to the employer, it may not be considered true reinsurance and could be subject to different regulations.

When discussing stop-loss coverage with clients, be sure to use clear, concise language and provide examples to illustrate key concepts. Encourage clients to ask questions and take the time to address any concerns they may have. By ensuring that your clients fully understand the role of stop-loss coverage in their Level-Funded plan and its implications for the plan's financial stability, you'll help them make informed decisions and build trust in your expertise as their broker.

Remember, your clients rely on you to be their guide in navigating the complexities of Level-Funded plans. By prioritizing education and transparency around stop-loss coverage and its legal nuances, you'll differentiate yourself as a broker who truly understands the intricacies of these plans and has their clients' best interests at heart.

These key terms and phrases form the foundation for understanding Level Funding. As you navigate through the book, keep these definitions in mind. They will help you grasp the intricacies of this innovative approach to small group health insurance.

Remember, mastering Level Funding isn't just about memorizing a glossary of terms. It's about understanding how these concepts interact and affect real-world scenarios. As you work with clients, take the time to explain these terms in plain language and provide concrete examples of how they apply to their specific situation.

By demystifying the jargon and making Level Funding accessible to a wider audience, you'll position yourself as a trusted advisor and thought leader in this rapidly evolving space. So dive in, absorb the knowledge, and get ready to revolutionize the way small businesses approach their health benefits.

THE LEVEL-FUNDING REVOLUTION

"How do you become successful? Very slowly, and then all at once."
— *Unknown*

L evel Funding is an innovative approach that blends aspects of self-insurance and stop loss coverage to offer small businesses (under 100 employees) control over their healthcare costs. It has the power to be disruptive to the traditional, fully insured, corporate health insurance model.

Level Funding gives employers the chance to function like their own insurance companies. They retain unspent claims money that usually disappears into the pockets of large insurance corporations at the end of each year. This possibility of a surplus changes the standard model. It offers small businesses the chance of a financial windfall, and responsibility linked to their employee's healthcare expenditure.

Early in my career, I experienced firsthand this method's impact. Out of the blue, I got a phone call from a small business owner I collaborated with the previous year:

"Tom, can you believe this?" he said, buzzing with excitement, "We just received a check for $158,000 from our surplus claims fund! I didn't think our health insurance plan could be so rewarding. Your guidance has been invaluable!"

I admit, I was surprised, even though I've always believed in the potential of Level Funding. The upfront savings we had already achieved were an indication that the concept could deliver long-term value for my clients. Still, receiving that surplus check marked a critical point in building solid trust.

In traditional fully insured corporate health plans, insurers keep any unused claims money at the end of the policy year. This happens even though the employers originally paid the premiums. Level Funding, on the other hand, allows companies to set up self-funded plans. In this setup, they have control over the claims pool.

Level funded plans work similarly to self-insured plans, as they are built on a self-insured model. Firms pay a fixed amount every month, designed to fund expected claims and administrative fees. The twist with Level-Funded plans is that they combine this self-insurance approach with stop loss coverage. This coverage acts as protection against unexpected, large claims.

Stop loss is crucial when individual or collective medical costs exceed certain limits. It caps the total liabilities for employers, creating a buffer against unexpected changes in healthcare usage.

In the mixed model, businesses have control over their plan design, claims processing, and any unspent healthcare funds. Yet, adding stop loss coverage can help limit the financial risk small businesses might encounter when relying solely on self-funded plans.

With accurate underwriting to predict expenses based on members' risk profiles, Level Funding can provide significant savings for smaller groups. What's more, if employees use less healthcare than predicted in a year, any unused claims money stays with the business. It adds to the company's cash flow if used to offset current plan expenses, instead of boosting insurance profits.

The surplus feature in our system repositions the priorities of stakeholders, promoting clever utilization of healthcare resources. It turns workplace wellness into an approach to boost returns, rather than just a method to slash corporate costs and incentivize workers. This fresh focus lets businesses and their staff come together and enjoy the benefits of wise use of resources.

A stronger sense of responsibility often guides better health decisions. Employees understand the mutual benefits of managing their healthcare plans effectively. This is because excess claims funds rarely go straight to the bank. If they did, they would be open to regulation and restrictions. However, if the money is instead creatively redistributed to the health and wellness of the company's employees, every penny can be put to good use. This includes wellness retreats, free yoga classes, or even paying into next year's claims costs so that they are lower instead of higher! As long as every employee benefits, surplus funds are essentially house money that everybody enjoys.

When employees share the benefits of surplus funds, they become more thoughtful in their healthcare spending. They reduce unnecessary trips to the emergency room and are more thoughtful about choosing dubious versus necessary diagnostic tests. Essentially, the approach of Level Funding discourages overuse and encourages healthier living choices.

Brokers selling Level-Funded plans stand out from commission-focused competitors. They don't have to center their work around income-based plans. Instead, they can tailor plans to meet the specific needs of their clients. The whole game changes with the introduction of the surplus feature.

Unfortunately for most brokers, grasping Level Funding isn't a walk in the park. It demands a considerable amount of learning. Brokers must grapple with complex rules while diving deeper into the specificities of reference-based pricing and stop-loss arrangements. The use of automated quoting tools meant for larger groups won't cut it here. Successful underwriting requires attention to detail and adherence to the brother rule.

Mastering this new approach takes time. Brokers may stumble as they learn how the right stop loss attachment points are set for each client. Jumping in without finding the right balance can lead to setbacks. But once brokers master the unique aspects of Level Funding, they can secure a strong market position. The payoffs? A distinctive way to stand out from the crowd, higher client retention rates, and massive amounts of referrals.

It's clear that aligning brokers' interests with their clients provides benefits. However, the traditional insurance models that focus on maximizing profits still dominate the small group insurance markets. Seasoned agents still struggle to understand how Level Funding can benefit groups of less than 100 employees. They're hesitant to embrace new systems that demand in-depth research and personalized underwriting, straying from their usual spreadsheet quoting tools.

Here, a little perspective can help. As a Spreadsheeter, it might take 20 minutes to an hour to provide a prospect a quote. But a practiced agent doing the work to offer a Level-Funded insurance plan might put in four to five hours of work. By comparison, this seems like a huge discrepancy. On the low end, agents offering Level-Funded plans work four times as hard! However, given the retention rates and downstream referrals of clients on Level-Funded plans, the question must be asked: how hard will you work today to not have to work in the near future? If you ask me, a hard day's work today for a lifelong client is more than worth it.

The success of Level Funding is all about the art and science of underwriting. It's about predicting costs accurately, providing both savings and stability. How do you forecast these expenses? It starts with a thorough look at health histories. Think medications, pre-existing conditions, likelihood of employees developing chronic illnesses, and their health habits. With detailed and reliable data, underwriters set the right aggregate and specific stop-loss attachment points.

Achieving flawlessness is never a simple feat. It involves a continuous process of experimentation and adjustment to identify optimal attachment points. But this effort is rewarding, helping prepare groups for potential surplus funds and spurring future referrals. Your portfolio's growth isn't purely dependent on your expertise; client satisfaction plays a significant role too.

As the wise saying goes, "Success is not final, failure is not fatal: it is the courage to continue that counts." Building a thriving book of business in the Level Funding space requires perseverance and a willingness to learn from setbacks. It's a journey of incremental progress, where each small victory paves the way for larger successes down the road.

THE SURPLUS MECHANISM: A CATALYST FOR CLIENT LOYALTY

"When incentives align, the burden and prize are shared."
— Unknown

A key advantage of Level Funding is the ability for employers to receive surplus funds if their employees happen to use less healthcare than expected in a given year. This surplus mechanism serves not only as a financial incentive, but also as a catalyst for building immense client loyalty rooted in shared success between broker and client. And it is this client loyalty that a young broker can build a solid and successful career on.

Receiving an unexpected surplus can deliver a rush of joy to a business owner. Imagine the thrill of a tax refund or an unanticipated inheritance. Even if the sums are small, the surprise of extra cash sparks happiness and leaves a lasting impression.

Imagine you're a small business owner, and you've just received a large check tucked inside a letter from your health insurance broker. This windfall is due to your team's commitment to healthy living, which kept them away from unnecessary trips to the emergency room. They didn't just save the company on insurance expenses, their prudence has also created opportunities.

Who's responsible for this win-win scenario? It's none other than your savvy broker who established your Level-Funded health plan! By doing so, not only do you enjoy reduced premiums, but your broker also contributes to your business's expansion in unanticipated ways. This creates a strong foundation of mutual trust and gratitude.

During the early stages of my career, I saw the significant effect of surplus funds. I was guiding a small manufacturer grappling with high health insurance costs. After I advised them, they switched to a Level-Funded plan, offering substantial savings at the outset. However, the owner doubted if this would be a lasting solution.

A year later, when it was time to renew, I couldn't wait to share some great news with our client. Their careful underwriting approach resulted in fewer claims than we expected, creating an $18,000 surplus. I suggested that we discuss whether he'd prefer the surplus funds forwarded to next year's expenses or would like to use them to improve employee benefits.

The business owner was thrilled. He was blown away by how the plan not only saved him upfront costs, but also returned a significant amount back after a year. The added benefit of choosing to either receive the surplus funds or reinvest them back into his business gave him a sense of control and ability to better support his team.

The plan's financial benefits brought a wave of enthusiasm. Watching the impact of the surplus mechanism play out, the owner became an ardent supporter of our services. Over the years he not only continued to be our client, but recommended us to a host of other colleagues.

This narrative exemplifies a consistent pattern. The surplus from an insurance plan transcends the simplicity of a refund. It instills a profound belief in the concept of "Level Funding." Skeptics are persuaded by the substantial promise of savings and stability, bolstered by a clear sense of obligation. Moreover, it evokes positive emotions, fostering robust bonds that extend beyond mere consumerism.

Within the business world, surprising your customers with unexpected wins is a proven strategy for generating referrals. Think about airlines that made headlines by giving away free flights—surplus funds can ignite the same kind of excitement. When customers receive unexpected "cash-back" from self-funded plans, brokers are seen as the heroes of the day. This inspires customers to share their successful experiences with their peers, positioning themselves as smart decision-makers.

As brokers, giving surplus funds helps us show clients the hidden value they gain from our expert advice. When clients hold their surplus checks, they experience firsthand the benefits of partnering with us, instead of settling for average vendors who might not have their best interests at heart. This transforms the broker-client relationship from a simple sales transaction into a profitable partnership rooted in shared gains.

Surplus funds build loyalty because they reinforce the relationship between brokers and clients. Brokers don't disappear after providing the initial insurance paperwork, like so many Spreadsheeters are akin to doing. Instead, Main Street Mavericks stay involved, advising their clients on smart ways to reinvest surplus returns. They lead them through the correct procedures after unexpected gains, making sure everyone follows the rules and regulations tied to insurance claims. By doing this, such brokers maintain open communication and consistently provide value beyond one-off deals.

When I began working with Level Funding, I made sure to reach out to every client as soon as their renewal information came in. We would discuss potential surplus funds, celebrate our shared achievements, and think about ways to enhance their benefits packages with the surplus. Many clients followed my suggestions, adding benefits like dental plans to keep their employees satisfied. Some even used the extra money to hold special events to appreciate their teams. All decisions served to reinforce our collaborative efforts.

Money wasn't the whole story. Using the surplus system, I kept in touch with my clients, demonstrating that I cared about more than their sale. I wanted to ensure their well-being year round. This consistent communication helped me earn my customers' trust. They were satisfied and ready to share their positive experiences, which brought me more business.

This strategy packs a punch. In the US business world, many health insurance brokers work for their commissions, disappearing until the following sign-up period. They're more interested in making a sale than providing ongoing service. But Level Funding changes the game. Brokers only win when they meet client needs by advising prudent usage. This shared benefit encourages responsibility, leading to plans that offer stability and personal care—elements often overlooked in traditional deals focused on minor savings.

In an industry packed with similar brokers battling for small savings, the ones who provide hefty surplus funds through Level Funding shine. They build customer loyalty, not merely through expertise but by being dependable allies in success. This generates an overflow of goodwill and referrals that money alone cannot purchase.

THE TRUE COST CALCULATOR*

This True Cost Calculator provides an estimate. All plans are different and calculations on specific and aggregate contracts are more complicated. Please contact marketing services.

CONTRIBUTOR SPOTLIGHT: TOM STEIN SR.

"Freedom is nothing but a chance to be better."

As one of the earliest champions of level-funding for small groups, Tom Stein Sr. has been a driving force behind the growth of this self-insurance model. He has been bringing self-insurance benefits to small employers for over four decades. Few can parallel his immense experience in the industry, but many can learn from his unique perspective on the challenges and opportunities of level-funding.

Tom first got involved in stop-loss insurance in the late 1970s, working for a company that was one of the pioneers in this space. At the time, self-insurance was still a relatively new concept, and was primarily used by large corporations with thousands of employees. But Tom saw the potential for this model to work for smaller companies as well.

"The VP of the department, a very bright guy, said we're going to get into the stop loss business," Tom recalls. "I'm thinking, well sure, what the heck is that?" After getting a crash course in the model, Tom went out and wrote the company's very first stop loss case. It didn't exactly go smoothly. "We only lost $100,000 on that one," he chuckles. "We were off to a great start!"

Despite this initial setback, Tom remained convinced that stop-loss insurance could be a game-changer for smaller employers struggling with rising healthcare costs. He began evangelizing the concept to anyone who would listen, working tirelessly to educate brokers, employers, and other stakeholders about the benefits of self-funding.

It wasn't an easy sell. Many brokers were skeptical of the idea, worried that self-funding was too risky for their smaller clients. They were used to the simplicity and predictability of fully-insured plans, and were hesitant to take on the complexity of a self-funded program.

But Tom persisted. He knew that with the right education and support, brokers could become powerful advocates for level-funding in the small group market. He traveled the country hosting seminars and workshops, sharing his knowledge and experience with anyone who was willing to learn.

Over time, Tom's efforts paid off. More and more brokers and employers saw the value in level-funding, and the model gained traction in the small group market. Tom's company became a go-to resource for employers exploring self-funding, and he became a sought-after speaker and consultant on the topic.

Looking back on those early days, Tom is proud of the role he played in bringing level-funding to the mainstream. But he's also quick to point out the job is far from done. As the healthcare landscape continues to evolve, he sees an ongoing need for innovation and education to help small employers navigate the challenges of self-insurance.

One of the key lessons Tom learned over his career is the importance of building strong relationships with brokers and employers. "This is a people business," he explains. "You can have the best products and the smartest underwriting in the world, but if you don't have the trust and confidence of your clients, you're not going to succeed."

To that end, Tom has always placed a high value on transparency, communication, and accountability in his dealings with clients. He believes that the key to success in the level-funding market is to always put the needs of the employer first, and to be a true partner in helping them manage their healthcare spend.

And to the need for ongoing education and professional development for brokers and underwriters, he notes, "This is a complex and constantly evolving industry. If you're not committed to continuous learning, you're going to get left behind." To support this need, Tom has been a vocal advocate for industry training programs and certifications, working closely with organizations like the Society of Professional Business Administrators (SPBA) to develop standardized curricula and best practices for level-funding professionals.

As he looks to the future of the level-funding market, Tom is optimistic about the opportunities ahead. He sees a growing appetite among small employers for more control and transparency in their healthcare spend, and believes that level-funding is uniquely positioned to meet that demand. At the same time, he acknowledges there are challenges on the horizon. Rising healthcare costs, regulatory uncertainty, and increased competition from new entrants to the market all pose significant risks to the level-funding model.

But Tom remains confident the industry will keep adapting. "We've come a long way since those early days of stop-loss insurance," he reflects. "But the fundamental value proposition of level-funding hasn't changed. It's all about empowering small employers to take control of their healthcare spend, and providing them with the tools and support they need to succeed."

For brokers and underwriters looking to enter the level-funding market today, Tom has some simple but powerful advice: "Focus on the fundamentals," he urges. "Build strong relationships with your clients, stay curious and committed to learning, and always put the needs of the employer first. If you do those things, success will follow."

This formula has worked for Tom Stein Sr. for over 40 years.

CONTRIBUTOR SPOTLIGHT: HOBSON CARROLL

As a veteran actuary with decades of experience in the self-funded health plan market, Hobson Carroll brings a unique quantitative perspective to the challenges and opportunities of level-funding for small groups. His insights highlight the critical role that sound actuarial principles play in designing and pricing these plans effectively.

After first becoming familiar with stop-loss insurance for self-funded plans of larger sizes in the late 1970's, Hobson encountered the product's extension to smaller groups working as the group actuary for stop-loss carriers in the early-mid 1980's. Given freedom to experiment with product variation and applying a primary concept from basic calculus to the question of what combination of product variables (attachment points and premiums) would minimize the maximum cost for smaller groups, he discovered some surprising, contrarian ideas to the classic marketplace approach to underwriting the typical specific and aggregate stop-loss of the day.

At the time, self-insurance was still a relatively new idea, and most employers who used it were large companies with thousands, or at least hundreds, of employees. Hobson remembers, "My insight from modeling and experimenting with different combinations of premiums and attachment points showed me that a different approach than the generally accepted market solution might work better for smaller groups, and the actual results of a couple of small beta-test blocks proved that to be correct."

"We knew it would be a challenge," Hobson recalls. "Small groups are inherently more volatile than large groups, which was, and is, fundamental knowledge. With fewer employees, there's more variability in claims experience from year to year, which makes it harder to predict costs for one group accurately even if you can do so for an entire book of such business." But, there were also similarities via a scaling viewpoint between how specific and aggregate experience for a book of business compared with a book of small group fully-insured business, lending additional weight to the development of a new approach.

"The idea was to have the employer take on more of the routine, predictable claims through a higher specific deductible, still capping their exposure on the really big, unpredictable individual claims," Hobson explains. "By structuring the plan design in this way, we could reduce the overall volatility and make the funding more stable and affordable for the employer so long as this higher specific was combined with an aggressively lower aggregate attachment point – that is the contrary result I mentioned earlier. Ultimately, by 1995, this led to the concept of using an aggregate only approach, and that was where the magic of small group level-funding was allowed to shine through in terms of being both competitive and sustainable."

Another critical factor in making level-funding work for small groups was the use of detailed medical underwriting to assess the risk profile of each group. While underwriting for any sized group needs to involve known group claims experience as well as community-wide demographic factors and actuarial manual rating, smaller group underwriting was hampered by the lack of credibility in such group experience, if it was available at all. Since an employer seeking a self-funded quotation was free of state or federal restrictions on individual underwriting like most fully-insured small group insurers had, and so were the stop-loss carriers and MGUs, individual health questionnaires could be utilized to protect the "block" of such business being developed.

"We looked at everything," Hobson notes. "Pre-existing conditions, prescription drug usage, prior claims—you name it. The goal was to get as complete a picture as possible of the group's expected claims costs, so we could price the plan appropriately and avoid any big surprises down the road. One of the primary keys to stop-loss underwriting is to avoid, or rate for, the known (or should be known) extra risk, and then getting an expected spread of risk across the entire book that you do write."

"Today, this approach of looking at anything that can further qualify the risk level of a prospective employer group has led to the advent of information-age augmentation data from social media and publicly or commercially available data collections, from which algorithmic modification to traditional actuarial risk underwriting projections is made," Hobson added. "The extension to utilizing fuller AI models cannot be far behind, but there I foresee challenges in terms of legal, regulatory, and perhaps ethical issues. Also, it is not yet clear that a true advantage can be gained. We shall see."

This granular underwriting approach required a significant investment of time and resources, and it wasn't always easy to get buy-in from employers who were used to the more hands-off nature of fully-insured plans. But for Hobson, it was a non-negotiable element of making level-funding work for smaller groups.

"We had to be really proactive in educating employers as to why this level of underwriting was so important," he explains. "It wasn't just about getting the best rate in year one—it was about making sure the plan was sustainable over the long haul, so they wouldn't get hit with big rate spikes or have to drop coverage down the road. Because this type of submerged aggregate level-funding product had more shared-risk corridor with other groups in the block, avoiding the extra risk was important to all the employers involved, and so it was worth the bit of additional effort involved."

Over time, Hobson's disciplined approach to underwriting and risk management began to pay off. His firm developed a reputation as a go-to resource for smaller employers looking to explore self-funding, and he became a sought-after expert on the financial mechanics of these plans.

In addition to his work on plan design and underwriting, Hobson also played a key role in developing tools and resources to help brokers and employers better understand the financial implications of self-funding. He created detailed financial models and projections to illustrate the potential savings and risks associated with different plan designs and funding levels.

"A lot of brokers and employers were intimidated by the

complexity of self-funding at first," Hobson recalls. "They were used to just looking at a single premium rate and not really understanding all the moving parts behind it. So, we spent a lot of time creating educational materials and tools to help demystify the financials and show them how it all worked."

One of the most useful tools was to model different claims scenarios and show employers how their costs could vary based on actual plan utilization. "It was really eye-opening for a lot of employers to see how much variability there could be in their costs from year to year," Hobson explains. "But by modeling out different scenarios we could help them get comfortable with that uncertainty and make smart decisions about how to manage it."

Ultimately, Hobson's goal was to help employers see self-funding not just to save short-term money on premiums, but as a long-term strategy for managing their healthcare spend and providing high-quality, affordable coverage to their employees.

"Self-funding is not a magic bullet," he stresses. "It's complex and sometimes risky. It requires a lot of discipline and expertise to do well. But for employers who are willing to put in the work and partner with the right team of experts, it can be an incredibly powerful tool for taking control of their healthcare costs and outcomes."

As he reflects on his decades of experience in the self-funding industry, Hobson is struck by how much the market has evolved and grown over time. What was once a niche approach used only by the largest employers is now a mainstream option for companies of all sizes.

But even as the market has matured, Hobson believes there is still room for growth and innovation. With healthcare costs continuing to rise and the fully-insured offerings less effective and sustainable as options, he sees self-funding as a critical option to retain.

For brokers and employers looking to explore self-funding today, Hobson has some simple but powerful advice: "Focus on the data," he urges. "The more you can understand about your group's specific risk profile the better you'll be in designing a plan that manages their needs effectively."

"Self-funding is not a one and done thing," he notes. "It's a dynamic, ongoing process that requires constant monitoring and adjustment to ensure the plan stays on track and continues to meet the needs of the employer and their employees."

THE PATH FORWARD FROM HERE

The Level Funding revolution represents a seismic shift in how small businesses approach health insurance. By offering a unique combination of cost savings, flexibility, and control, Level Funding plans empower employers to take charge of their healthcare spend and provide better benefits to their employees.

But as with any disruptive innovation, the path to widespread adoption is not without its challenges. Brokers who choose to specialize in this niche must be prepared to invest significant time and energy into educating themselves and their clients about the intricacies of self-funding. They must be willing to challenge the status quo and face resistance from those who are comfortable with the way things have always been done.

However, for those who are up to the task, the rewards are substantial. By becoming true experts in Level Funding and building a reputation as trusted advisors, brokers can differentiate themselves in a crowded marketplace and build lasting, profitable relationships with their clients.

The key to success in this field is a combination of technical expertise, strategic thinking, and a deep commitment to putting clients' needs first. It requires a willingness to listen, to educate, and to adapt to the ever-changing landscape of healthcare.

As we look to the future, it's clear that the Level Funding revolution is just getting started. With rising healthcare costs and increasing dissatisfaction with traditional insurance models, more small businesses are seeking out alternative solutions that can provide better value and more flexibility.

For brokers who are ready to seize this opportunity and lead the charge, the possibilities are endless. By embracing the role of innovator and advocate, they have the power to reshape the small group health insurance market and make a real difference in the lives of the clients they serve.

Your Secret Sauce

"An ounce of prevention is worth a pound of cure."
— Benjamin Franklin

Underwriting plays a key role in crafting custom Level-Funded health plans that offer a competitive edge over traditional fully insured corporate choices. By carefully anticipating a company's healthcare expenses determined by their unique risk profile, brokers can create plans that provide considerable upfront savings and potential surplus funds over time. However, excellent underwriting demands thorough data collection and analysis.

As a rookie, I struggled with tight profit margins. One of my first groups was a small landscaping company with 26 employees, an ideal case for self-funding. I managed to secure a contract from a big national carrier, offering slightly better benefits at lower premiums. But I soon realized that my hasty predictions missed crucial details, messing with my claims assumptions.

The reality hit hard as the plan's real expenses exceeded our estimates, resulting in a staggering loss ratio of over 110% by the end of the year. It was clear that my plans needed more than just a few tweaks to the pricing to stay viable. The strain was palpable in my business relationships as well, as they were burdened with the weight of unfulfilled expectations. My flawed underwriting abilities cost me dearly, including my reputation and trust with clients and partners alike.

My early failure taught me a valuable lesson about the importance of thorough underwriting, especially for smaller groups operating with small profit margins. I realized the importance of gathering four times more health history data, despite resistance due to the increased work. Our actuaries had developed innovative rating algorithms that factor in variables like generic medication preferences and local heart procedure rates. We updated our systems to automatically flag any unusual metrics during data upload, ensuring any strange data received an instant review.

This disciplined process resulted in an impressive level of accuracy. Our loss ratios in the first year were much closer to the initial targets on average. These improved predictions allowed us to reduce rate thresholds, knowing that the risk of large claims was acceptably low. The result? Our premiums became more competitive, and our customers enjoyed larger surplus checks.

Underwriting empowers brokers to shape plans to match each organization's goals. Gathering detailed data provides a clear view of each employee's health status. With this information, brokers and TPAs can expand benefits for essential services and reduce unnecessary ones. For instance, if we spot many type-II diabetes cases, we can bolster prescription coverage and make the broker aware of digital weight loss programs, instead of supporting less relevant smoking cessation initiatives. Knowing the workforce's lifestyle steers wise investments in wellness programs that clients appreciate.

In short, thorough underwriting unearths chances for strategic plan design and vendor integration tailored to specific needs, rather than enforcing generic solutions for the masses.

Winning the underwriting game boils down to three key steps. First, it's important to collect detailed health histories of all employees. It's not just about identifying obvious conditions like asthma or diabetes, but also about understanding each person's prescription medication use, allergies, and past medical events, no matter how small. All this data plays a crucial role in refining loss forecasts.

In the second step, underwriters give scores to people based on factors they can control that may impact their healthcare use. They consider things like how well they manage their weight, their sleep habits, and whether they smoke or use controlled substances. These measures help identify those who might push up costs and those who could foster a more health-conscious, cost-effective environment. With this data, we can design tailored programs that promote healthier lifestyles. Companies can use these scores to inspire their employees, tying reimbursements to better health choices that match the company's big-picture goals.

The last step involves surveying employees to understand how culture affects healthcare spending. We look into behaviors like regular interactions with healthcare providers, which could increase healthcare usage. The survey also identifies outdated beliefs which might encourage unnecessary or aggressive treatments. It's not just about physical risks related to the job—the survey gives insight into the collective mindset of employees. This crucial information can guide investment in education to ensure optimal healthcare consumption.

A thorough underwriting review in areas like individual health risk and lifestyle behavior lets self-funded programs offer tailored plans to small employers. It lets us step away from outdated assumptions used in setting rates and puts leaders in control of costs and the distribution of unused claim funds. If you ask me, this is an enormous step-up from inflexible insurance plans.

Good underwriting reflects dedication to the client relationship. Small business owners know when a consultant is considering both their immediate needs and long-term goals. Top agents use their underwriting insights to recommend Level-Funded plans, setting themselves apart from those who rely on rate calculators. By focusing on accurate loss predictions, brokers highlight their expertise and role as advisor. This positions them as dedicated risk partners whose success is tied to the policy's performance.

The initial investment in this hands-on method pays off significantly over time. Once you master superior underwriting, referrals start rolling in, reducing the need for lead hunting. With a steady flow of renewal revenue and strategic consulting, growth opportunities will be within your reach. By stepping beyond simple spreadsheeting, you transition from just another sales agent to a respected advisor who holds sway in business leadership. This transformation begins with a commitment to master superior underwriting. The positive impact you make more than justifies the effort you invest.

SMALL BUSINESSES AS MINI-INSURANCE COMPANIES

"When you know the numbers you take better action."
— Unknown

Level Funding offers a unique advantage to small businesses. It lets them behave almost like their own insurance company, keeping a firm hold on their healthcare costs. This isn't achievable with traditional fully insured plans. With Level Funding, these businesses can craft health plans that align with their risk profiles and benefit needs. They go ahead to set deductibles, coinsurance rates, and preferred provider networks based on their specific needs. If there are unspent healthcare dollars at the end of the policy term, these businesses get to keep the surplus, just like an actual insurance company would.

Imagine you're a homeowner with a plan to revamp your kitchen.

You want new cabinets, countertops, and appliances, with a budget of $20,000. You have three major options to get this job done:

Option #1 is akin to a traditional fully insured health plan run by a big national insurance company. The company assembles a one-size-fits-all plan with network, formulary, and identical coverage tiers across all possible customers. It's simple with minimal effort for the buyer. But the company keeps any savings as profit. In other words, you get predictable results while paying most (if not all) of your budget.

Option #2 represents the self-funded approach. The homeowner (small businesses) take ownership of plan design and can custom-build superior benefits matching their needs and sensibilities. Acting as a mini company puts them in the driver's seat, allowing them to capture gains from prudent utilization—same as carriers. Becoming champions of their own plans allows customization impossible through general contractors focused on broad serviceability. So, while the homeowner puts in all of the work, the results are more aligned with the desired outcomes, and the costs are better maintained.

Then there is Option #3, a hybrid approach where the homeowner (the business) shares responsibilities with a general contractor. This is akin to Level Funding. In this setup, the homeowner is in charge of buying materials and managing the workforce. The contractor, meanwhile, provides technical guidance and expertise. This option is a sweet spot, providing the best of both worlds. On one hand, the homeowner has control over their budget and can save some money. On the other hand, they can rely on the contractor's know-how, which can be invaluable, especially in complex projects. Better yet, if there are any extra supplies at the end of the project, the homeowner may repurpose or sell those materials to recoup some of the upfront costs.

The business environment is ever-evolving, and small companies need to stay on par with growing expectations around benefits, despite resource constraints. Level Funding presents a solution, empowering leaders—who interact regularly with their staff—to attract and retain talent. It offers choice on a more manageable scale. But first, there's a need for a shift in mindset—moving from resigning to the inevitable to exploring the possible.

Level Funding presents a unique approach to handling healthcare expenses for small companies by offering control, flexibility, and the potential for savings. Rather than handing over vast sums of money to large insurance providers without guarantee of fair returns, these businesses can function as their own mini-insurance providers, retaining any savings gleaned from efficient health management.

Level Funding's appeal is its flexibility over traditional health plans. These old-school plans often serve large Fortune 500 companies well, but they can ignore the needs of smaller groups. Level Funding, on the other hand, is ideal for niche organizations that need custom solutions. It aligns well with startup cultures that value independence. Plus, any savings can be channeled into growing the business instead of padding the bank accounts of insurance companies.

This model hands the reins of controlling crucial facets of the health plan to the company. The facets are:

- **Custom Plan Design:** The company sets the rules like deductibles, rates of coinsurance, and provider networks. They create these rules based on their budget and needs. This flexibility is a great alternative to the rigid boundaries of fully insured plans.
- **Clear Claims Picture:** In a self-funded or Level-Funded plan, the company has a clear view of all claims made and their costs. This insight allows companies to manage their spending and track usage trends more effectively.
- **Surplus Opportunity:** If employees use less healthcare than expected and there's leftover money, the company gets a surplus at the end of the year. This is a significant perk compared to unused funds going straight into the insurance company's pockets.

To make a Level-Funded plan work, though, business owners need to see themselves as more than just insurance customers. They need to see themselves as designers of personalized plans that boost their talent strategies. And it's the broker's responsibility to help shape this perspective.

At no point is the agent's role more important than in the handling of a surplus check.

Remember, when starting a conversation after providing a surplus, be careful. Most business owners' instinct is to take the money as extra income. But that takes the money out of the protection of ERISA non-ERISA laws, which means it may be taxed. Always encourage people to speak with their tax attorney. A more strategic use of the funds not only provides better support to the business, but also increases the impact of every dollar.

Steer the chat toward the business owner's long-term objectives, not just the immediate financial benefits. "We're in an unusual situation with extra funds in your plan's claims account. Rather than making a hasty decision, let's look at options that fit your long-term business goals." Pose questions, throw around ideas, and imagine— how can these funds help growth or improve employee loyalty?

When you are more creative with the use of a surplus check, you increase your value from broker to business advisor. Most business owners won't think to use the surplus funds to lower future premiums, add company benefits, or fund a company retreat. When used wisely, surplus funds can provide immediate relief, a future safety net, and a vessel for accelerated growth. Help your clients see the potential rewards of smart investments.

After talking to your client, it's time for the referrals to start rolling in. Except, this doesn't happen automatically. As willing as happy clients are to provide referrals, they often need a little prompting. In other words, ASK.

Handing over a surplus check is a golden opportunity to ask satisfied clients for referrals. By strategically asking for introductions to other business owners while celebrating a mutual financial success, you can attract potential clients while they're still riding the wave of positive feelings. When a company receives an unexpected surplus from their claims, they often feel a sense of gratitude toward their broker. This feeling makes them more receptive to further suggestions. In this positive atmosphere, asking for referrals feels less like a hard sell and more like a natural progression. That being said, there is a method I've learned to follow that usually generates success.

First, I want to cultivate client loyalty by celebrating the surplus check in person, not just delivering it in the mail. Then, I try to highlight the emotional connections established by the company's financial win. And finally, I broach the topic of a referral in a conversation with a seven step strategy. Let's break these all down.

CULTIVATING CLIENT LOYALTY THROUGH SHARED CELEBRATIONS

"You bring the balloons, we'll provide the check."
— *Publishers Clearing House*

A surplus check from a Level-Funded health insurance plan can be a unique chance to build stronger bonds with clients. It's a shared moment of financial triumph that can pave the way for lasting relationships that surpass single transactions. Celebrating such a big moment for a company is too big an opportunity to pass up. So, initiate it.

I can distinctly remember an early client of ours, a small home insurance agency. They were savvy with their claims, keeping costs well under our predictions, and ended up with a notable surplus. Hearing the news of his incoming surplus, the owner, Sam, was absolutely thrilled.

Instead of mailing the check, I thought a personal touch would make it more memorable. So, I created a moment to celebrate the accomplishment. His agency was based in Richmond, Virginia, so I flew out to hand-deliver the check over dinner at a high-class steakhouse. I also brought a carefully selected gift—a framed vintage picture with his agency's first offices in the foreground.

As soon as I arrived, Sam welcomed me with a heartfelt hug. He showed genuine gratitude for our services, and others in attendance also chimed in, celebrating their company's success. This sense of accomplishment belonged to all, not just Sam. Over dessert, Sam declared his plans to use the surplus money for a summer staff picnic catered by a top-notch restaurant. He saw it as a unique opportunity to thank his team for their dedicated efforts to keep claims low. Tying rewards to team commitment in this way earned him a round of applause from everyone present.

The mood was vibrant, and I asked Sam if he was aware of other home insurance groups or business partners facing trouble with their corporate plans. I suggested that we might be able to assist them in considering self-funding. Sam responded positively and mentioned several names.

Choosing to celebrate the surplus news personally instead of just mailing a check helped us solidify a genuine relationship with Sam's agency. It wasn't just business. We created an emotional tie around a notable event. This honest and open approach led to referrals.

Client surplus funds are special opportunities. Rather than merely providing checks, brokers are wise to organize memorable moments. But the aim must be more than a tedious accounting meeting that goes through boring numbers. Throwing a party to celebrate a surplus windfall doesn't have to be complicated. It could be as easy as handing out branded merchandise to show your thanks. But if you take the time to personalize these events based on what your clients like, you can build stronger relationships. So, learn more about your clients. Find out about their hobbies, favorite foods, dream vacations, family life, and passion projects. Use this knowledge to create experiences that resonate with them emotionally.

The payoff in referrals will be well worth the cost of time and money.

HIGHLIGHTING EMOTIONAL CONNECTIONS THROUGH FINANCIAL WINS

"Aligning incentives isn't just about short term gains. It's about creating a roadmap that guides individuals toward shared objectives, keeping them motivated and interested in the adventures ahead."

— Unknown

The most potent benefits of surplus checks are the emotional ties they foster among leaders and their teams. When you encourage leaders to recognize the people behind the surplus and not just the data, their rewards become more personal than a simple gift card. Your partnerships will feel more intimate because you are creating a new and powerful way for their teams to bond.

If given the opportunity, you can magnify the scope of your impact with a thoughtful speech. When you highlight your values amid an emotional celebration, you can further connect the moment to the bigger picture. Sure, the business you're supporting has experienced a win, but so has the Level Funding revolution. Don't miss the chance to capitalize on serious momentum by connecting your clients to what's happening beyond their company doors.

The best way to help businesses associate their accomplishment with a higher purpose is to come prepared with stories. When you're about to give a surplus check, first share about how other clients effectively used their surpluses. For example, you could talk about a struggling business that upgraded their vital equipment thanks to the extra cash flow. Or, illustrate how one client enriched their employee benefits plan with more life insurance, courtesy of the surplus claims dollars. These motivating tales can trigger ideas about the potential of strategic reinvestment.

When you highlight the greater impact of the surplus, the individuals that make up the company will begin to connect their financial win to the greater community. They'll see how the dollars kept in their business will benefit their families, their schools, and their local economy at large. By highlighting these emotional connections, you turn a savvy business strategy into a meaningful use of company resources. Suddenly, those individual employees may start to wonder...*What other small businesses can benefit from a self-funded plan, and therefore further benefit the community?*

By engaging people in fun, creative, and emotional ways, these events can help communities use extra funds to kickstart widespread improvements. Over time, these communities can achieve healthcare independence one event—and one company—at a time. They can form powerful grassroots partnerships that go head-to-head with major carriers. Celebrate that!

ASKING FOR REFERRALS

"A referral is a way of borrowing someone else's credibility."
— Unknown

A surplus check presents an amazing opportunity to a business. But while it is the realization of progress for the company with the insurance plan, it is only the beginning of work for you. This might sound crazy after you've spent nearly two years hustling for clients, qualifying them, setting them up, and then advising them in their use of their policy. However, unless you want that work to be representative of your entire career, then you must recognize that your most important work has just begun.

If you know how to ask for referrals during the time when you have the highest probability of success, then you can look forward to a future where you spend less time prospecting and more time closing new business. So, how do you capitalize on your opportunities to ask for referrals? To increase your odds of getting a top-notch referral, follow these steps:

1. **Time the request appropriately:** Wait until the initial shock and celebration peaks before making your ask. Let the client revel in their surplus first. Then pivot the positive mood into an ideal moment for your appeal.

2. **Frame the success collaboratively:** Reinforce that the surplus resulted from teamwork between you and the client's staff to prudently manage healthcare resources. Share credit for accomplishments.

3. **Offer authentic appreciation:** Express genuine gratitude for the trust placed in your guidance and the daily diligence by their workforce in making such impressive outcomes achievable.

4. **Note additional service capacities:** With emotions elevated and business leaders feeling highly favorable toward your performance, highlight your high potential value to other companies.

5. **Make recommendations visual:** Provide pamphlets, flyers, or brochures during this interaction showcasing your breadth of specialized services. You want decision-makers to have handy takeaways so that they keep your solutions top of mind.

6. **Ask directly:** Pose a concise request for a set number of three introductions to colleagues and connections who might similarly benefit from assessing their current health plan arrangements. Give them a card with three blank lines to fill out.

7. **Follow up diligently:** During the days that follow, personally connect with every single referral, as well as the team you just delivered a surplus to.

Take advantage of these opportunities by getting in touch with clients as soon as you know the surplus amounts. Don't hold off until it's time for renewal talks. Recognize their team's smart use of resources, which resulted in the surplus. Next, prepare for future discussions. I use a semblance of the following script:

"We've teamed up and accomplished something notable. The plan had a good year, resulting in surplus funds due to prudent claims management. No doubt you've got ideas on how to put this money to use. How about we schedule a call to talk about those ideas and think about introducing some extra benefits?

"As I reviewed our records, I observed an interesting pattern. Many of your vendors and partners don't have a full benefits package. Considering the value these partners add to your operations and your commitment to the local community, they might welcome our unique approach. Who do you think would most benefit from Level Funding?"

Then stop talking and wait quietly.

This method gently eases into the subject of referrals. We present it as a chance for peers to benefit, not a hard sell. It ties to the client's beliefs in supporting partners and the broker's talent in crafting tailored solutions. The right phrasing often makes the client eager to introduce new prospects.

The timing and tone are key when you're asking for referrals while handing over checks. Celebrating early sets the tone for mutual benefits. When you ask for referrals in the right way, it feels like sharing beneficial solutions rather than making unwelcome cold calls. Being considerate shows respect for both the referrer and the potential client.

Naturally, maintaining strong relationships and earning referrals require a solid reputation as a dependable advisor. Your past work and established partnerships are what encourage clients to recommend you to others. Remember, trust and demonstrated expertise attract more interest from peers than any slick sales pitch. The most valuable referrals come from years of dedicated service where you have proven yourself as a steadfast ally.

Use the Right Bait

Now that you understand how Level Funding works, and why proper underwriting is the secret sauce that makes it all happen, let's dive into the details. In the next few chapters we're going to walk step-by-step through the process of finding clients, attracting them to your offering, pitching them on Level Funding, and signing them up. The sales process for Level Funding is particular—you don't sell it the same way you sell any other type of health insurance.

The process is like fishing. I'm an avid fly fisherman. There's nothing I love more than finding a secluded fishing hole and whiling away an afternoon pulling trout or bass out of the water. I've come to realize that the qualities that make someone good at Level Funding sales are virtually identical to the qualities that make someone good at fishing.

If you want to catch fish, the first thing you need is…a place with fish. And this can be tricky to find. You can't just go fishing in the same place as everyone else. Those spots are all fished out. Finding a good fishing hole is an art in itself. It takes curiosity, persistence, and ingenuity. But when you find the right one, you've overcome one of the biggest hurdles already.

Once you're in the right spot, at the right time of day, the next question is what to use for bait. I wouldn't spend so much time learning how to tie different flies if it didn't matter what was on the end of my line. You have to notice what types of insects are common in the area. What are the fish eating here? And what is something that might look to be an exotic treat for them? All of this, of course, is a metaphor for prospecting.

Perhaps the most important thing you can do to guarantee success on your journey to build a book of business in Level Funding is to make sure you're talking to the right people and you're offering something they want. You can't fish in the same place as everyone else with the same bait everyone else is using. So put on your waders, grab your tackle box, and let's see how to find the perfect fishing hole for prospecting leads in your area.

The first rule is that you need to find hungry fish. Level Funding isn't for all small businesses. When introducing something as groundbreaking as Level Funding to the health insurance marketplace, it's essential to pinpoint the businesses that can benefit significantly from this method. The first step in reaching out is to identify businesses that are currently facing urgent issues that you can help resolve.

Consider a broker I once knew, we'll call him Steve. Steve faced a number of challenges when selling comprehensive corporate plans to small construction companies. The risky nature of construction work, along with thin profit margins, left these businesses vulnerable to harsh rate increases. These increases hampered their ability to retain their employees. As the company grappled with expensive premiums and rising deductibles, their employees moved on to better opportunities, leaving construction timelines in chaos.

Every time Steve tried to offer alternatives to these construction company owners, they brushed him off. They had the notion that all brokers were the same—handing out rate sheets at job site trailers and then disappearing until it was time to renew. Why would they sacrifice their valuable time to listen to yet another cookie-cutter sales pitch?

Steve needed a way to show he was deserving of these companies' time. So, he decided to attend local construction association meetings, where he could meet the business owners in person and build rapport. Then, instead of pushing sales, he offered pointers and insights to help the companies out. He hosted friendly cookouts, gifted tools to emerging apprentices, and even held seminars on identifying common workplace hazards.

It was only a matter of time until the next increase in health insurance rates reignited existing frustrations within the local community. So, when Steve brought up Level Funding, business owners were primed to listen. They trusted Steve, and were open to a new approach.

Next thing Steve knew, he not only had a number of business owners eager to sign up, but they recommended him to more of their struggling colleagues. His credibility helped them overcome their uncertainty, and the relationships he formed turned out to be more valuable than simple transactions. He no longer had to rely on persistent cold calls for business. Instead, based on his reputation for delivering practical solutions, people sought him out.

This tale underscores an essential point: instead of using up resources trying to attract random prospects, it's smarter to focus your primary outreach on groups urgently seeking change. Every market has subsets grappling with particular stressors, always on the hunt for solutions. By aligning unique remedies with clusters feeling the heat, you make strategic targeting more impactful. In other words, find yourself some hungry fish.

The best initial prospects for self-funded plans typically fall under these categories:

- **Small businesses seeking insurance.** Many owners of such businesses desire to offer insurance coverage to their workforce, but find the traditional fully funded insurance options pricey. With Level-Funded plans, they can manage to provide insurance.
- **Companies struggling with high employee turnover.** If a business is losing staff because of a lackluster benefits plan, self-funded plans might be the answer. These plans can be tailored to improve the benefits package, making it more appealing to employees.
- **Companies experiencing rapid growth, particularly startups.** A sudden surge in staff can lead to rising insurance premiums, which can put a lot of financial pressure on a company. Level Funding, which bases its premiums on current enrollment and not outdated data, can help lighten this financial burden.
- **Businesses with younger, healthier workforces.** Younger teams often face inflated insurance rates. Level Funding can be a game-changer for these companies. It rewards them for promoting healthy lifestyles among their employees.

Certain groups bear more burden than others under existing corporate plan structures. We can address these specific challenges by tailor-making our marketing and promotions. This way, we can share success stories of people who've triumphed over similar obstacles. When prospects see we understand their situation, they'll be more interested. Custom approach beats generic advertising.

Let's be clear: Level Funding isn't a cure-all for every small business scenario. Declaring it as such might harm your reputation. So, make certain any potential clients fit into these categories. Focus on finding business owners who could significantly benefit from what you have to sell. Don't waste your time trying to catch fish that aren't hungry.

Your search must be more specific than just anyone who owns a business. Reach out to targeted trade groups, local associations, and professional networks. Find members who fit the profile of the perfect Level Funding prospect. Sponsoring booths at their events is more worthwhile than at unrelated community festivals. Contribute to their publications, discussing common issues and offering simple solutions. By addressing the insurance troubles plaguing small and medium-sized businesses, brokers can start useful discussions.

By analyzing and ranking groups using concrete data that indicate their likelihood to use our solution, we can eliminate guesswork. This approach allows us to allocate our resources effectively. Our decisions must be based on solid evidence rather than mere theories.

Even when you target the right companies and industries, your conversion rate won't improve without the right approach. When first selling Level Funded plans, new brokers tend to be overeager. The problem here is that people will push back when they feel imposed upon. However, they might show interest if you provide insights into their unique concerns. In this situation, a broker's introduction seems less of an imposition and more of an invitation. A well-crafted message can transform an interruption into an opportunity.

In insurance, unspecialized sales rely on high volume due to low profit margins. Brokers often accept any customer without seeking the ideal match. However, with Level Funding's intricate nature, brokers need strong partnerships from the start. Identifying unsuitable candidates early saves time. Not everyone is suited for self-funded plans or enticed by potential savings. Brokers must avoid hastily implementing Level Funding universally before mastering service to specific segments.

Let the need for change guide your engagement strategy. Stick to your standards and take your time. When traditional options no longer cut it, alternatives start looking good. But don't waste effort trying to educate a disinterested market. Instead, focus on market segments that are ready for change and show potential for Level Funding. This approach can speed up sales, lower acquisition costs, and link the product with those most likely to adopt it.

RIPE OLD BANANAS

"In Japan, they call it Muda, or waste. The beauty of entrepreneurship lies in the ability to see potential where others only see byproduct."
— Unknown

As a young health insurance agent seeking to grow your book of business, where do you start? One of the most powerful strategies at your disposal is to focus on ripe old bananas—those leads that have been discarded or overlooked by other brokers as too much effort for too little reward. These warm prospects, properly cultivated, can become the cornerstone of a thriving book that catapults you to the top of your field.

Where does the saying "ripe old bananas" come from? Pre-World War One, there was a teenager who escaped the Russian Empire and came to America. And he went to the most booming city in America he can think of: Biloxi, Mississippi. He doesn't speak a lick of English, but he rolls up his sleeves and gets to work. After a few years of working odd jobs, the now 19-year-old boy has saved $30. Remember, this is pre-WWI, so compared to today that would have been about $1,000. And what does this hard-working industrious boy do with his money?

Well, it helps to know what Biloxi was known for in the early 1900s. On the Gulf of Mexico, Biloxi was one of the primary shipping destinations for bananas. On any given day, shipments from the United Fruit Company, one of the largest corporations on the planet, would line the docks with boxes of the fruit. Before the bananas were shipped onward, though, they were separated into two piles: ripe bananas and unripe bananas.

The unripe bananas were prepared to ship onward because they were less likely to go bad on the journey. But the ripe bananas were thrown away. By the time they reached a destination up the East Coast, they were likely to be old and rotten. So, to the shipping companies, the ripe bananas were trash.

But to our young hero, these piles of ripe bananas contained hidden treasure. Before the ripe bananas could be thrown away, he purchased as many ripe bananas as his $30 could buy. A whole rail car's worth. And as he loaded up his rail car, he paid some friends in bananas to message ahead to North Mississippi: "Tomorrow, there will be bananas on the stands at a discounted rate. This is a limited time offer, you better buy what you can."

That night, he slept on the railcar as it traveled to North Mississippi. When he arrived, the stands were packed with people ready to buy. Within minutes he sold every banana. And just like that, he stumbled upon a business model that turned United Fruit Company's trash into a thriving business enterprise.

The moral of the story? One person's trash is another's treasure. The key is having the vision to spot hidden value where others only see spoilage. In the health insurance world, ripe old bananas often take the form of small businesses that have been ill-served by the traditional fully-insured market. These are the employers who have endured double-digit rate hikes year after year with little explanation or relief. The mom-and-pop shops who have been told that they're too small to underwrite profitably. The startups who have been forced to choose between gutting their benefit offerings or going out of business.

These beaten down buyers have grown jaded from seeing their health plans treated as an afterthought by brokers chasing sexier mid-market accounts. They've been conditioned to believe that annual premium increases are as inevitable as death and taxes. And they've all but given up hope of finding an advisor willing to invest the time needed to understand their needs and craft a creative solution.

That's where you come in. As a level-funding specialist, you have the power to show these neglected niches that there's a better way. By taking the time to perform detailed health risk assessments and tailoring plans to the unique profile of each group, you can deliver immediate savings and a path to long-term stability that will make you an instant hero.

But it's not enough to simply wait for these ripe old bananas to fall into your lap. You have to proactively seek them out. Here are some tried and true tactics for finding and capitalizing on these hidden gems:

Within your personal and professional network, there exists a wealth of potential clients. Consider individuals such as your uncle who owns a small plumbing business or your college friend who launched her own marketing agency. While they may currently be clients of larger brokerage firms, it is likely that they are not receiving the personalized attention and innovative solutions that they merit. Arrange coffee meetings to reconnect and guide the conversation toward their benefits challenges. Subsequently, impress them by demonstrating how your boutique, service-oriented firm is ideally suited to cater to their specific needs.

Partner with centers of influence. Local business groups like the Chamber of Commerce or Rotary Club can be treasure troves of warm leads. Instead of just showing up to monthly mixers with a stack of business cards, take the time to build genuine relationships with the chapter leadership. Volunteer for committees and panels where you can demonstrate your expertise. Offer to teach a workshop or sponsor a lunch-and-learn on the unique health insurance challenges confronting small companies. Over time, you will become known as the go-to authority in the business community on employee benefits. And when members inevitably come to the chapter heads for referrals, guess whose name will be at the top of their list?

Get creative with your marketing. Instead of leading with mind-numbing insurance jargon, focus your messaging on the real-world pain points these neglected niches face. Empathize with the frustration of double-digit rate hikes, the headache of parsing pages of insurance gobbledygook, the fear of not being able to attract talent with subpar benefits. Then paint a compelling picture of how Level Funding can be their salvation, with clear language and relatable case studies. Leave the steak dinner seminars to the big boys—your scrappy ripe old bananas will respond much better to a grassroots marketing approach.

Double down on referrals and testimonials. Once you've helped a few ripe old bananas see the light with Level Funding, be sure to transform them into vocal advocates for your business by consistently asking for referrals and testimonials. These real-world case studies from similar employers will carry far more weight than any slick brochure or fancy website. Make it easy for happy clients to sing your praises by providing ready-made email templates they can use to introduce you to industry peers.

And ALWAYS follow up with a heartfelt thank you for an endorsement, no matter how small. Referrals are a transfer of trust, and that is very personal.

At the end of the day, prospecting ripe old bananas is about seeing possibilities where others only see pitfalls. It's about understanding the unique needs in the abandoned corners of the market. The Russian immigrant who turned that one nearly spoiled shipment of fruit into a banana empire didn't succeed by following the crowd. He saw untapped potential where others only saw trash. And then he busted his rump, innovating ways to extract and deliver that value against all odds.

BEFORE CUSTOMIZING PLANS, CUSTOMIZE ANALOGIES

Introducing Level Funding to small business owners requires careful explanation of its advantages over conventional plans. Though the chance of getting a surplus at the end of the year is appealing, the initial steps involve accepting more responsibilities and risks. Getting business owners to feel at ease with this approach depends on clear communication about how Level Funding aligns with their objectives.

My encounter with a small landscaping company's owner really drove this point home. When I first introduced the concepts of self-insurance and stop-loss arrangements, he was overwhelmed. Terms like "laser deductibles" and "aggregate attachment points" felt like a risky, expensive foreign language to him.

Noticing his confusion, I switched tactics. "Your business thrives because you've mastered the art of cost efficiency while providing excellent service—and that's why your customers stay," I explained. "Now, imagine if you applied the same principle to your healthcare costs through Level Funding. It's like buying bulk fertilizer for a big discount or using high-tech mowers to save on labor. And by analyzing your staff's data, you could negotiate better rates based on usage—similar to better underwriting. It's all about cutting costs wisely, using strategies you're already familiar with."

As the idea clicked, his puzzled expression gave way to understanding. "Why didn't you start with that?" he laughed. By relating complex health insurance terms to his everyday business operations, I helped him to see the value in the Level-Funded approach. This sparked a discussion about choices, where simple comparisons turned tricky concepts into real-life examples for him.

Breaking down complex ideas can help simplify intricate plans like Level Funding, making them more understandable to the layperson. The trick is to avoid baffling jargon and specifics that might cause your audience to lose interest—even if they really want to comprehend the subject. Using easy-to-understand examples, offering straightforward comparisons, and highlighting the benefits can keep their interest and gradually broaden their understanding.

During a project with a small auto repair shop owner, I gained some new insight. Rising costs from his current corporate insurer frustrated him. I proposed a Level-Funded approach that offered more control and the potential for surplus refunds. However, he hesitated.

"I just need to provide coverage, not underwrite insurance," he explained. "My team is already swamped with invoice management. Now, you want us to handle insurance risks too?"

I had to explain Level Funding to him in a context he understood. I used the analogy of bulk buying car parts—the more you purchase, the cheaper each part becomes. I asked him if he considered his garage's expenses when buying inventory. Then, I made a connection between studying claims at his shop and his insurance planning, using the same bulk buying principle.

After linking his business operations with health coverage planning, his initial worries started to subside. At last, we found common ground. When he understood how Level Funding mirrored tasks he already handled, his uncertainty morphed into curiosity. We discussed ways he could use surplus funds to reduce cost, boost team spirit, or cushion rates against market changes. By linking the plan to specific goals, I helped him see its benefits more easily. Soon enough, he was confidently explaining self-funding to his skeptical office manager.

This business owner's story demonstrates how a successful education about Level Funding can make it valuable to clients. While possible surplus funds are appealing, the extra tasks of plan administration might scare off clients. It's essential to be patient when introducing additional risks and responsibilities.

Think back to the world of fly fishing. We're selling all the fish on biting the same exact hook. But much of the art of being good at fly fishing is in the creativity of how you tie your flies. We develop these elaborate knots with all different colors and shapes to mimic different types of insects that the fish might find interesting. We have to notice what the fish are responding to in each different region and think about the best way to present the hook so they'll be enticed to bite.

In the world of health insurance sales, the "hook" we want the prospects to bite is the idea of Level Funding. But how we present this idea to the prospect can vary significantly from one industry to another. We have to tailor our approach so that we are using language that will appeal to the prospect. And I have found the most effective way to do this is by developing metaphors and analogies that put the idea of Level Funding into a context that immediately resonates with the prospect.

Let's see how we can break down Level Funding into simple terms and pair it with examples that are easier to understand. You could relate self-insurance to common business practices, such as buying in bulk or budgeting based on past spending. You could also explain reference-based pricing using examples from vendor contract negotiations. Think of stop-loss insurance as a warranty that covers unexpected equipment breakdowns, going beyond normal wear and tear.

Using examples that make sense to the listener is a great way to break down complex ideas and keep business owners engaged. This method makes complicated information feel less daunting and reassures them that they can grasp these new concepts without getting confused. Regularly check in to ensure they're on the same page, and let them dictate the speed of the conversation to avoid bombarding them with unfamiliar terms.

Using language that resonates with business owners can foster a sense of understanding and connection. By tailoring your communication to their specific industry and terminology, you create an environment where they feel heard and valued. This approach sets you apart from those who rely on generic language or complex jargon, which can alienate prospects and make them feel like outsiders. When you speak their language, you demonstrate your comprehension of their challenges and aspirations, nurturing a foundation of trust and building rapport.

OVERCOMING THE FIRST HURDLE

"The confused mind always says no."
— Unknown

Once you find the right types of business owners, earn their trust, and pitch Level Funding to them using just the right language, you'll reach the first major hurdle on the path to closing a new client. This is where you'll have to reveal that getting started with Level Funding is a lot more work than a traditional health insurance plan. The truth is this is not only more effort for the sales rep, it's also a lot more work for the business owner. This quadratic work ethic applies both ways.

Unlike standard rate sheets that simply need a signature, Level Funding requires underwriting diligence, compliance monitoring, and reporting management. All these tasks take more time than a typical fully-insured plan.

It is important to be upfront with prospects about the added effort involved in walking this path. Don't try to downplay the fact that this is more work. That will only lead to resentment later on as prospects feel misled. Instead, be honest and let the prospect know that all of the advantages of Level Funding, along with the potential for a surplus, do come with a cost. And that cost comes in the form of additional leg work during the approval and set up process.

Often this conversation will begin naturally as skeptical business owners ask you, "What is the catch?" We've all been conditioned to know there's no such thing as a free lunch. The immense benefits of Level Funding can, frankly, sound too good to be true. It is common for business owners to ask the rep, "What are you not telling me?" At this point it can actually be helpful to have an answer in your back pocket: setting this plan up is about four times more work.

Here's where lifelong learning comes into the mix. I assure business owners that we can shoulder much of their burden with our third-party administrative services (TPAs). We've proven ourselves with clients in similar situations. I firmly think that the extra mile is worth the long-term savings, added control, and possible surplus funds. If we can successfully underwrite a fitting Level-Funded program after reviewing their employee health histories, and they choose to partner with us, I commit to tackling the challenging bits for free. I'm dead set on finding the best solution for their business.

Being willing to do the initial groundwork for a long-term partnership changes how we view the extra efforts needed for Level Funding. Instead of shying away from more work, savvy business owners see this commitment as proof of a broker's real intent to meet their specific needs, rather than just selling generic plans. By showing I'm prepared to go the extra mile to provide custom solutions, I can change early doubts into keen interest. I do this by promising that together, we can navigate complex tasks to achieve goals that go beyond simply cutting costs.

So, if handled properly, this first hurdle can turn into a springboard for your broker-client relationship. When prospects realize that you're offering to put in a significant amount of extra effort on their behalf because you firmly believe this plan will be better for them, it solidifies the trust you've built up to this point. This further establishes your role as a trusted advisor rather than a mere vendor.

In a field crowded with brokers simply clocking in for their commissions, those who take on extra work with no guaranteed returns (albeit, tons of potential returns) stand out. They demonstrate a keen interest in producing exemplary results. Seeing these efforts as a testament to commitment, not just an obstacle for closing deals, builds faith in beginning the process of due diligence required for self-funded programs.

EXTRA WORK DEMONSTRATES COMMITMENT

"Action > Talk"

Of course, this isn't just more work for the business owner, it's also more work for you, the sales rep. Just as the added effort on the prospect's end can be beneficial when phrased in the right way, the extra steps you'll have to go through as a sales rep also pay off down the line. This process will force you to learn the ins and outs of the prospect's business and understand the healthcare requirements of every individual on their team.

Moving a small business to a Level-Funded health plan means more upfront work for the broker than selling a simple corporate policy. Detailed underwriting and collecting thorough employee health data is hard. Still, it lays the groundwork for precise predictions that assess the plan's practicality. Above all, it shows the broker's commitment to putting the clients' needs first.

My dad, seasoned health insurance broker that he is, imparted the significance of meticulous underwriting to me. As I embarked on my journey selling plans, I attempted to streamline the process with succinct employee questionnaires. This was aimed at accelerating enrollment. However, Dad pushed for detailed documentation of every employee's medications, health conditions, and medical records, even if it meant making countless extra phone calls.

He would often say, "This is how you foster trust." By putting in extra work at the start, you show that your aim is to provide long-term support, not just to chase after quick gains.

I remember when I landed my first client, a plumbing shop. I spent a month collecting employee health data which, while tedious, really impressed the owner with my thoroughness and dedication. I delved into everything, from chronic illnesses to an employee's preference for generic drugs. My thoroughness showed the owner I was more than just a salesman, I was a dedicated business partner. This approach laid the foundation of a lasting partnership.

When fly fishing, there is a practice called catch and release. Many non-fishers have heard of it, but few actually know the rules for determining which fish you can keep and which fish you have to throw back. There are certain criteria fish have to meet for you to be able to legally keep a catch. If they're too small, too large, or a type of fish that is out of season, then you have to release the fish back into the wild.

The last thing a professional angler wants is to get in trouble for an illegal catch. Depending on the state, fines can cost upwards of a thousand bucks for a fish. Certainly not worth the catch. And if the angler wants to maintain a rewarding pastime, he will need a system for ensuring every catch he keeps qualifies as a fitting catch.

The same is true for your level-funding prospects. You might have the most eager business owners in the world, but if their companies don't qualify for Level Funding then you might have to release them back out into the wild.

To make accurate predictions about healthcare costs and design practical Level-Funded programs, it's crucial to collect detailed employee data before quoting potential clients. This involves delving into the details of medications, along with any pre-existing medical issues, and past or recent medical procedures. It also means considering lifestyle factors such as eating habits, smoking tendencies, and use of alcohol or other substances.

Collecting this information can be difficult, but it's crucial. Missing even one health issue or medication can mess up future plans. Full transparency from the start fosters trust and avoids unexpected setbacks after approval.

Business owners might initially resist the idea of detailed underwriting, especially if they're used to the less intensive methods used by corporate plan brokers. It's also possible that some employees could feel uneasy about sharing their medical information. Remember to prioritize their privacy and take time to reassure any hesitant individuals that their confidence is more important than simply finalizing a deal.

If anyone hesitates to conduct an underwriting, be cautious. Neglecting to analyze risk properly can lead to shaky quotes, often requiring later adjustments. This damages trust and credibility. A commitment to detailed initial data collection is a safety measure that benefits everyone in the end.

Even the most thorough underwriting might miss a few issues that only become apparent later. But taking the time to gather as much information as possible at the outset forms a robust foundation. This way, you capture over 90 percent of the factors that enable accurate loss modeling. Conversely, rushing through an underwriting increases the chances of unforeseen issues. Detailed due diligence helps maintain stability by identifying potential risks and preparing for them.

If you're a broker just starting with Level-Funded plans, the idea of a detailed underwriting might feel a bit overwhelming. You could even see it as pointless compared to corporate quotes that are easier. You might question why you would pour in your time and energy with no promise of clients bringing in a good return on your investment, even if the underwriting goes through. Sure, gathering this data requires some elbow grease at the start, but the payoff is substantial.

If you're keen on delivering top-notch healthcare solutions for small businesses, comprehensive underwriting is key. Advisors trying to stand out through deep expertise and relationship-building will find this an excellent chance to shine. A hands-on approach builds trust, showing clients that their advisor can handle complex issues beyond basic rates. This method, focused on consultation rather than quick fixes, also builds loyalty.

Over time, clients start to appreciate the benefits of better-aligned programs and stay loyal. This loyalty spreads through word-of-mouth referrals, all thanks to advisors who prioritize clients' well-being over making quick sales.

Mastering this challenging task builds confidence among groups navigating the unknown terrain of Level-Funded plans, which rely on predictive data for success. But the end goal isn't just to prove technical expertise. Showing dedication to essential, but less glamorous, tasks sends a strong signal. It shows you are committed to helping their organization succeed through servant leadership. This kind of dedication garners respect and recommendations that can fuel considerable growth for your book of business.

Never underestimate the power of attention to detail. The key is to see every employee as more than a statistic. They're an important piece of a larger web of connections within the company. Real people bank on these plans, and your attention to detail directly affects their future. This perspective paints a vibrant picture of colleagues.

Setting Realistic Expectations: Not Everyone Qualifies

"Even houses in deserts have gutters."

Shifting a small business to a Level-Funded health insurance plan can be a long journey, and approval isn't always a sure thing. Brokers who support this model need to be upfront about the odds of qualifying to establish trust with potential clients.

I first learned the importance of honesty while advising a small consulting firm interested in self-funding. After our first chat, the partners wanted to know if such a plan could work for their modest-sized company. I told them Level Funding could work for small businesses, but it would depend on the health profiles of their employees.

The first thing we did was collect a comprehensive medical history from each partner. But the health information we collected highlighted myriad health risks. Several partners had serious health conditions that required specific treatments and medications. One was waiting for knee surgery. Complicating matters further, the son of one partner was receiving treatment for leukemia. So, the potential for claims was too large to match with reasonable insurance rates.

I suggested a high deductible policy paired with a health reimbursement arrangement (HRA) to match their health risks. However, partners were hesitant to assume potential liabilities. Their existing concerns about profits made them cautious. As sharp business minds, they appreciated my candidness about the risks beyond their control. We agreed to part ways in a friendly manner, looking into other options instead of pushing an unfit Level Funding policy on them.

My experience shows that managing expectations for approval, no matter how a broker may push the positives of self-funding, is a crucial part of the job. It's true, Level-Funded programs can bring some liabilities and might be more unpredictable than fully insured plans. They're a great fit for groups that are generally healthy and use their plans wisely. But for businesses struggling to stay profitable, or those with risky profiles, adding self-funding to the mix can be a wild card. This uncertainty often turns away potential candidates, regardless of the broker's zeal or the company's potential savings.

Consider these common reasons why certain groups might not qualify for Level Funding:

- Medical histories or pre-existing conditions
- Certain expensive medications
- High risk professions
- Upcoming medical procedures
- Financial instability

When I talk about Level Funding with potential clients, I'm quite frank about the limitations. About one out of five or six groups applying don't meet the criteria, often due to inherent risks or intentional deceptions or misrepresentations that go against the rules of self-funded plans. I encourage transparency during these talks. That way, any past issues come to the surface early, sparing them the fallout of unexpected surprises later on that might jeopardize their credibility.

I find sharing hard truths from the start useful. It gives potential clients an honest look at the proposal, rather than letting them believe everything will be smooth sailing. I emphasize that even if they're not eligible at first, they could still qualify in the future by adjusting their habits. By discussing these limitations openly, we pave the way for smarter choices instead of unexpected surprises down the line.

While revealing these constraints may discourage potential clients, keep in mind that strict underwriting is the goal for the model's long-term survival and steady growth. It's wiser to avoid unpredictable situations. Strong programs that meet strict criteria are the priority.

THE REWARD: CEMENTING LONG-TERM RELATIONSHIPS

"The fundamental glue that holds any relationship together is trust."
— Unknown

Transitioning to a Level-Funded health insurance plan for a business can seem daunting with its extensive requirements and complexities. But when you manage to navigate through it all, you come out with a solid, trust-based relationship with a high likelihood of mutual success.

One of my early clients was a manufacturing firm, Acme Titans (name changed for privacy). I worked closely with Acme's leadership team for a few months. Our task list was extensive. We collected detailed employee underwriting data and prepared conservative loss predictions based on their risk profile. We also secured stop-loss coverage and completed all the paperwork for their Level-Funded solution.

The journey was tough, requiring focus and perseverance from everyone involved. Doubts and obstacles emerged regularly and, three weeks in, Acme's leaders questioned if we'd ever complete the process. Still, I remained steadfast, aiming to reveal the control and flexibility Level Funding could offer. And when the plan was approved, the look on some employees' faces as they received their new insurance cards was a spectrum of shock and disbelief.

After we introduced Acme's improved benefits package and smart utilization management, it didn't take long for the anticipated cost savings to start rolling in. But what really got people talking was the buzz during the first open enrollment. We saw over 90% participation from employees, who happily shared their positive claims experiences. Even the CEO was impressed, confessing, "You addressed all my worries and I'm thrilled to see my team happy!"

Fast forward eighteen months, and it was clear we'd succeeded. Our focus on effective care coordination and wellness tactics at Acme helped us drastically reduce costs. We even managed to avoid touching our stop-loss coverage. As the plan year ended, I was thrilled to share this news with our leadership team. Our initial loss estimates were so conservative, we found ourselves with a surplus of $72,000!

Handing the surplus check to the leadership team felt like a joyous celebration. The path had been a rollercoaster, but this moment meant more than just business success—it touched everyone on a personal level. The CEO embraced me and said, "I put my faith in you last year, and you have shown us why it was the right decision." In the warmly lit conference room, the line between advisor and client became blurry among proud colleagues. Our bond was deep, strengthened by our united determination against challenges.

I benefited heavily from commissions, and they saw gains in their balance sheet, but the benefits didn't end there. A quiet loyalty was growing between our two organizations. Both of us were invested in mutual growth, having weathered the upstart together. Better yet, I got referrals. And the confidence of the companies Acme Titans referred me to made future upstarts easier. There was less hesitancy from business owners and employees during the underwriting because they were coming to me.

Not every project or client relationship is smooth sailing, but when advisors steer organizations through the rough waters of a transition, a strong bond forms. This bond grows stronger from working together to find solutions. Early wins might seem like luck, but real bonds endure through challenges, standing firm against time and market changes.

It Starts with a Handshake

At this point in the process you have found a reliable source of high quality leads and you've developed a way of communicating your value proposition with prospects so that they get it and they feel you are aligned with them. Before you go racing off to collect detailed employee medical histories and begin the underwriting process to deliver them a quote, there is a critical step that you can't miss. We need to entice the prospect to make a commitment. We need their word that if we do the extra work to run all of their employees' medical histories and we are able to successfully underwrite the plan that they will go ahead with the process and sign up.

In the world of fly fishing, after we find the right spot, tie the right fly, cast our line, and get the first bite, we need to set the hook before we can reel the fish in. If we start reeling before the hook is deeply set, we have a good chance of losing the fish. Maybe they were only nibbling at our hook and weren't really serious about taking a chomp on it. I have lost a good many fish this way in my time.

While setting the hook on a fishing trip is a rather forceful maneuver, getting a commitment from the prospect in the world of health insurance sales is much more subtle. We don't want the prospect to feel cornered or trapped. At this point, they should be excited to give us their commitment. But how we seek that commitment is very important. If we do it wrong we can scare them away just at the moment when we almost had them on the line.

Many approaches to sales use a Letter of Intent (LOI) at this point to secure a commitment from a prospect. This might involve typing up a somewhat formal email that lays out the proposed partnership and asking the client to affirm or even sign the document. The LOI typically specifies that the prospect is serious about the possibility of doing business together and that if everything checks out the way the sales rep hopes, the prospect is ready to move forward with the engagement.

In the world of health insurance sales, however, I have found that a much more subtle approach is actually more effective. This business, as we have seen, is built heavily on trust and relationships. Since we have been working to earn the prospects' trust and we have already begun building a relationship with them, we can leverage that trust to gain their commitment. The process to achieve this isn't complicated at all. In fact, it can be done in seconds with a simple handshake.

The power of the handshake deal as a method of achieving buy-in from trusting business partners is not to be underestimated. When you shake the hand of someone you respect and look them in the eye and give them your word, that means something. Even in today's world of virtual relationships and doing business over Zoom, the handshake still holds an almost mythical power. I have found that a simple handshake at the right time can make the difference between closing a deal and losing a prospect.

It was early in my career, in a completely different business, that I first experienced the awesome power of a handshake. I had joined forces with a small Amish furniture maker, selling items like rolling pins and cutting boards made from local, environmentally friendly wood. Our business thrived on trust, with large custom orders agreed upon over a handshake during our weekly meals together.

Now, growing up with a father in the insurance business, I inherited a mindset of always thinking about everything that could potentially go wrong. I couldn't believe these guys did massive business deals with a shake of the hand. What if something doesn't go as planned? Didn't they want to specify all the terms of the engagement and get it all in writing? How could they hold someone to their word in a court of law if there was no record of the agreement that had been made?

The wooden appliances business really started to take off, and I secured a deal that I thought would solidify my success. We sold a massive order of Knightstands to an upscale chain of stores called Brookstone (not their real name, to avoid getting sued). These were finely finished wooden bedside tables with a quick-access gun safe hidden in the back. They wanted thousands of dollars worth of Knightstands and were committing to renew the order every quarter for three years. It was by far the biggest order we had ever received. In fact, this single contract quadrupled the size of our business overnight.

Hardly able to believe my good fortune, I raced off to ramp up production to meet this new demand on an accelerated timeline. I procured a massive order of specialty wood and urged my Amish collaborators to put the operation into overdrive. I told them I would buy as many Knightstands as they could make. And, of course, they nodded and we shook hands. My business had made multiple payments to the Amish workers in the past, so there was some established trust. The deal was done.

Soon after we shipped the initial batch of Knightstands to Brookstone and acquired a new shipment of premium hardwood, we received distressing news: Brookstone declared bankruptcy. They canceled all future orders and were unable to fulfill payment for the Knightstands we had already completed. This left me in a precarious financial situation. I owed tens of thousands of dollars and was in possession of a significant quantity of expensive wood without any immediate purpose.

At this point in my life I was a struggling kid trying to get a business together. I had spent everything I had to fulfill the request from Brookstone, because it seemed like a sure thing. When the order evaporated into thin air I was left with nothing. It was a massive punch to the gut. What was I going to do? How would I continue the business? And, most importantly, how would I ever pay back the Amish for everything I owed them?

Shaking with fear, I knocked on the door of my trusted friend, the Amish woodworker. I laid it all out for him—the unexpected contract cancellation and my inability to pay him as promised. In response he simply stated, "Tom, what can you do now?"

I proposed a potential payment plan to resolve the issue sooner rather than later, and we shook on it.

"Thank you," I said.

He just nodded and replied, "I know you'll make it right."

His free, unquestioning trust surprised me. Although businesses often crumble under stress, this behavior was both humbling and inspirational. It fostered a bond far more robust than any contract. In return, I did my best to support his workshop. His trust not only helped me through a rough patch, but also opened new doors within his network when I did "make it right," ultimately giving my growing business a significant boost.

The irony of the whole situation is that I had a firm dozen page contract in place with Brookstone and in the end it meant nothing. Whereas the Amish and I had nothing more than our word and a simple handshake. In the end, that proved stronger and more meaningful. Now, years later, I have done all kinds of business with the Amish. Our relationship has grown and deepened over time. And I never did another deal with Brookstone or any of the people there ever again.

Trust fosters loyalty, often surpassing legal obligations. While safeguards are vital, strategic openness can spark generosity and strengthen organizational unity. In healthcare discussions, a timely handshake can ensure long-lasting loyalty.

Let's Shake on It

"Shared incentives are a superpower."
— Charlie Munger

Securing a verbal agreement from hesitant clients at the onset is key. This agreement transforms the underwriting process into a joint venture. It draws the customer into the mutual pursuit of solutions. Suddenly, you're not just a zealous salesperson promoting a plan for a profit. Instead, you're a part of a co-operation focused on achieving distinct goals.

New brokers often hesitate to invest a considerable amount of unpaid time into prospects who might eventually back out. If this happens, they're left with lost time, broken promises, and no income. But, overlooking the hard work as merely a cost of entry disregards a crucial point. This dedication can transform tentative prospects into enthusiastic supporters. When customers see a broker putting in weekend hours for thorough underwriting without immediate profit, they begin to trust. Undecided customers perceive that only a confident broker would invest such time and effort. This visible dedication becomes a selling point.

However, you're not going into your unpaid weekend work hours without any sense of security. This is where the all-important handshake comes in. You're going to make a miniature deal with the prospect. You are offering to do a bunch of extra work on their behalf to analyze their employees and get them approved for the plan. In exchange, they are offering their assurance that if you are able to get them approved for the plan, they will go ahead with it.

Here's what I tell prospects: "If I do this work and can show you how Level Funding is your best option, do I have your business?" If the answer is "yes," then we shake on it.

While many aspects of business can be done digitally today, and even important conversations can happen over video conferencing, this particular exchange must take place in person. What really makes the handshake work is grasping the other person's hand, looking them in the eye, and asking them to give you their word. It only takes a few seconds, but it is critical. This is not something that can be done through a computer screen.

What we want to avoid is the situation where you do all the research, gather the employee questionnaires, perform the underwriting, put together the custom plan, and present it to the business owner only to have them decide not to go forward. Doing the extra work to put together a Level-Funded plan is only worthwhile if the prospect actually signs up for the plan you produce.

Don't shy away from the extra work, but also don't be afraid to make a demand in exchange. You've already given the business owner a lot of value by this point, and now you're about to set out and do a bunch more work on their behalf. At this stage of the sales process, you haven't asked the prospect for anything yet beyond some of their time for conversations. Now is when you need to make that first ask. And if you are unable to secure a commitment from the prospect, you must respect your time enough to refuse to move forward.

It is possible the prospect is unwilling to commit at this point. Maybe they say they need to see the quote first before they can commit anything. This is not something that you can accept. You don't have to be a punk about it (in fact, I never recommend being a punk), but you must secure a commitment from the prospect before you proceed to the underwriting phase. If they are not ready to supply that, go back and build more trust with them. Educate them better on the intricacies of Level Funding and explain in more detail why it is better for their business. Continue to nurture the relationship over time. Position yourself as more of an expert. Do whatever it takes to get that commitment, but absolutely do not move forward without it.

The commitment phase in selling health insurance is crucial. Once you receive the handshake, the client will begin to trust you like a business partner. Now you both have some skin in the game, even if they haven't paid you any money yet. By shaking your hand, they have invested themselves in the relationship and in the process.

With this handshake in your back pocket, you've now got the prospect opted into your sales process. The fish is on the line and the hook is set. They aren't going to swim away after you go through all the effort of preparing a specially curated plan. So, now you're ready to move into the actual heavy lifting of performing your research and underwriting the deal.

THE FOURFOLD WORK ETHIC

"Diligence is the mother of good luck."
— Benjamin Franklin

As I have mentioned throughout the book, switching a business to Level Funding demands more initial work than opting for a traditional fully insured plan. I often use a metaphor called "The Fourfold Work Ethic" to illustrate the level of dedication necessary to provide comprehensive underwriting. And that work ethic must kick in right after the handshake.

The idea of the Fourfold Work Ethic came about from the realization that Level Funding is four times more work than standard fully-funded insurance. But I have also come to think of it as encapsulating the four pillars of thorough underwriting.

First, the diligent agent will take a deep dive into our potential clients' employees' health histories. This means contacting each employee to collect a detailed record of their medical and prescription histories. We work harder than our competitors, showing our dedication to creating the most precise plans with meticulous underwriting.

Second, we aim to enlighten business owners about the crucial role accurate predictions play in their plan's durability and potential savings. This involves illustrating the need for a comprehensive initial evaluation for Level Funding. If we don't keep reminding the prospect of why all the extra work matters, they might get fed up with the process halfway through. During this stage, we address any concerns, and highlight the benefits of a highly tailored plan.

Third, we work to keep the prospect focused on the future. While your broker is working on underwriting the plan, speak with the prospect about their company's growth plans for the next half-decade or so. The goal isn't just to shave off a few dollars in cost from their budget, but to look at bigger aspects too. Talk about how benefits can help boost staff retention, make them a top choice for potential hires, and enable them to pour funds into tech upgrades to fuel growth. Position yourself as someone who can design forward-thinking plans and be a steady guide toward the business's long-term success.

Finally, you want to work on keeping the prospect informed about the status of their plan approval process, sending regular updates about what's next so they're never in the dark. Be overly communicative. Keep them in the loop about everything that is going on behind the scenes. And celebrate the little victories, helping to keep morale high during the necessary but often monotonous regulatory stages. After all, this is exciting!

The key to all aspects of the Fourfold Work Ethic is excellent communication with the prospect and their team. Avoid the urge to deflect questions about progress with vague promises. We've all felt dubious about the all too common excuse, "There are complex procedures happening behind the scenes." Instead, offer detailed updates about finished tasks, challenges to tackle, and strategies for upcoming obstacles. View every question as a chance to educate decision-makers about evolving regulatory rules, turning them into active contributors.

Our goal is to build a culture of total transparency. Keeping an eye on developments at every step and communicating each little win with the client can make Level Funding seem less like a mysterious plan formed in secret. We aim to break down and clarify each part, allowing customers to play a crucial role in crafting their programs. The more they engage, the better they understand the process. This is why the paperwork of underwriting a plan is only one fourth of the Fourfold Work Ethic it will take to succeed.

Patience is key as you work through this process, particularly for new clients unfamiliar with Level Funding or the approval process. This is your opportunity to create stronger connections than you would if you were merely a vendor. Prospects value regular communication and they respond positively when you get excited about your mutual successes. As the process moves along, look for opportunities to update them with good news.

Recognizing the value of incremental, step-by-step objectives is key to pulling off big projects. It might feel odd to dream of towering skyscrapers when you're just laying basic foundations, but keep working to connect the daily tasks of the underwriting process with the bigger dreams that motivated your prospect to get started with the process. By leading steadily and celebrating small victories, you can create a deep bond that gets you through hard times later on.

By adhering to these four principles, we help our clients to view the effort we put in as a testament to our commitment, over just chasing a paycheck. This changes their perspective on brokers—from simple product sellers to essential companions dedicated to building long-lasting relationships. Going the extra mile earns trust and word-of-mouth recommendations over time, even though the immediate returns might be hard to quantify. The future is paved for those willing to take the initiative, without the assurance of immediate pay-offs. Progress calls for perseverance in the face of uncertainty. It's a challenging venture, but it ultimately pays off for those who embark on it with determination.

LONG GAME STRATEGY: EDUCATING CLIENTS ON PROCESS COMPLEXITY

"The obstacle is the way."
— *The Dao De Ching*

You might have noticed that much of the effort involved in the Fourfold Work Ethic is focused on communication and education, not simply stacks of paperwork. Crafting Level-Funded plans isn't just an exercise in crunching numbers, it's about building relationships. Much of what you'll need to do during this phase is based in managing the human elements of the sales process. It's about navigating sensitive conversations with employees and making them feel comfortable disclosing their medical history. It's about engaging prospects and managing their expectations.

I learned a valuable lesson from an interaction with Walter, a seasoned executive leading a rapidly rising startup in the crypto realm. Given the limited expertise available in cryptography, he used unique perks to attract exceptional developers. When I proposed a custommade, Level-Funded plan to give his company an edge, he eagerly agreed.

Walter's initial excitement quickly cooled when I mentioned that the paperwork and approval process could stretch on for months. "My startup isn't like a slow corporation tied up in bureaucracy. It's fast-paced and needs to adapt rapidly to changing conditions. I was hoping for more innovation from this self-funded plan, and less red tape," he responded.

I told Walter that every step of this legal process was crucial. We were dotting our 'I's and crossing our 'T's to prevent any future legal issues. Naturally, he wasn't ecstatic, but he agreed to proceed. However, as our process was continually delayed for additional research, Walter's irritation grew. With the volatile nature of the cryptocurrency industry, our insurers insisted on a cautious approach and extensive risk assessment.

Walter vented his frustrations to me over text, hinting at the enormous pressure building within his HR team. They were drowning in a sea of employee questions. These communication breakdowns were a ticking time bomb for our business deal, mainly due to an underestimation of the process's complexity.

I invited Walter to a meeting where we could realign with our long-term goals. Yes, the situation was challenging, but we needed to understand and adjust our system before fine-tuning it. I presented the approval delays not as hindrances, but steps toward creating a unique model. This model could attract high-quality talent in the future. By viewing these challenges as key steps in perfecting our solutions, we adjusted our timeline expectations. Walter agreed, letting out a sigh. "You're right, Tom," he said, "System changes aren't quick or easy. We have to keep our eyes on the goal."

So, we stuck with the deal. Walter's team, known for their determination and innovative thinking, kept going despite the hurdles. Our imaginative solution reflected their pioneering spirit and became part of their journey. Sixty days later, we sealed the deal.

This tale underscores the importance of setting realistic expectations when dealing with Level-Funded plans. Indeed, the approval process can be long, sometimes startling entrepreneurs and small business owners. But, viewing these obstacles as stepping stones toward innovation can help alleviate stress. It's crucial to understand that following rules today can set the stage for tremendous benefits in the future. Present the necessary steps as keys to unlocking future breakthroughs that more traditional firms may not access. Show how overcoming today's challenges can lead to tomorrow's opportunities.

Simply put, guide clients like Walter to adjust their perspective. Encourage them to prioritize long-term growth, which paves the way for future success. Instill in them that legal clearances aren't discouraging obstacles, but rather, they distinguish the true innovators from the reckless ones who lack the concentration to responsibly transform complex systems. Depict Level Funding not as a mere cost-cutting measure, but as a stepping stone to acquire the sophistication needed to revolutionize employer health plans.

The health plan approval process takes time for good reason: to ensure compliance and prevent later issues. Rather than surrendering to frustration over red tape, take satisfaction in crafting foolproof, ethical plans methodically. Let stringent requirements test your team's mettle, molding them into empowered innovators who refuse to let short-term administrative hurdles impede their grand vision. Establish careful foundations now, so you can swiftly develop bold innovations in the future, the kind that risk-averse competitors wouldn't dare attempt without demonstrating the disciplined integrity you've exhibited. Let's embrace the process and regulation as milestones of lasting industry leadership while playing the long game.

CLIENT LOYALTY BEYOND NUMBERS

"The only two things that matter in life are trust and time. Everything else is for sale."
— Tom Stein Sr.

In the cut-throat world of health insurance, clinching long-term customer loyalty isn't simply about showcasing numbers on a spreadsheet. It's about fostering trust-based relationships, delivering stellar service, and celebrating shared victories. This personal touch can turn you from just another vendor to an irreplaceable partner. The underwriting process is not easy, but that also means when you make it through the challenge, there is a mutual feeling of success. You and the prospect walked through the fire together and made it through victorious! This cements a lasting bond between you and the client. The importance of this is not to be underestimated. Years down the line your relationship will likely be tested.

I recently experienced just how important these relationships are when a small manufacturing firm, a client of mine for several years, was approached by a competitor. As we were preparing for their plan renewal, I received a phone call from the owner, Bill.

"Tom," he started, "I value our partnership, yet another broker has offered big savings if we shift our plan."

Instead of getting upset, I realized Bill's responsibility to explore what was best for his staff and business in the long run. I suggested setting up a meeting to discuss strategies to enhance their employee benefits package and fine-tune our service. Bill agreed to my proposal.

Susan, a member of my team responsible for wellness initiatives, accompanied me on our call the following week. This was crucial given Bill's emphasis on his employees' health and engagement. Susan spelled out the exciting wellness advantages we could provide by using the savings from our low-cost plan. These benefits involved gym memberships, healthier cafeteria options, and the launch of summer Fridays.

Bill looked pleased as our meeting wrapped up. Giving my hand a firm shake, he said, "Tom, it's clear you genuinely care. You're not just focused on profits, but on my employees' wellbeing with these added benefits." To Bill, my personalized approach meant more than fluctuating premium rates. I'd earned both his trust and his business."

I learned from this experience that gaining loyalty isn't just about cutting costs for clients. It's about aligning with their values too. By giving Bill's company the personal touch that they couldn't get elsewhere, I showed them my commitment. Unlike my rivals who only boasted about lower premiums, I gained trust by focusing on building a significant relationship. Those months we spent together back at the start of our relationship, working through the intricacies of the underwriting process, created a bond that I could fall back on when other insurers tried to steal Bill from me as a client later on. You can bet I was glad that I had put in the effort upfront.

Contributor Spotlight: Steven Schouweiler

As a seasoned veteran of the self-insurance industry, Steven Schouweiler has worn many hats over his long career—underwriter, consultant, broker, executive. But the role he is perhaps most passionate about these days is that of educator and mentor. For over a decade, Steven has been at the forefront of training and developing the next generation of self-insurance professionals, with a particular focus on the rapidly-growing market for smaller self-funded groups.

Steven first got involved in self-insurance education back in the early 2000s, when he was working for a major stop-loss carrier. At the time, large employers dominated the self-funded market with thousands of employees and sophisticated benefits teams. But Steven saw an emerging opportunity in helping smaller employers access the benefits of self-funding through innovative product designs and risk sharing models.

The problem, he quickly realized, was that most brokers and advisors serving these smaller employers had little to no experience with self-funding. They were used to simply spreading insured premiums from the fully-insured world and lacked the technical underwriting and plan design expertise to structure a self-funded plan.

To address this knowledge gap, Steven started developing training programs to teach brokers the fundamentals of self-funding, from claims analysis and reserving to stop-loss contracting and risk management. He traveled the country hosting workshops and seminars, slowly building a grassroots network of brokers and advisors who were hungry to learn about this new funding model.

Over time, those initial training efforts evolved into a more formal educational infrastructure. Steven worked with industry groups like the Self-Insurance Institute of America (SIIA) to create a standardized curriculum and certification for self-funding professionals. He also began partnering with TPAs and stop-loss carriers to offer ongoing education and professional development to their broker partners.

The response from the broker community was overwhelmingly positive. For many, these training programs were their first real exposure to the world of self-funding, and they appreciated Steven's ability to break down complex concepts into practical, actionable insights. They also valued the opportunity to network with other like-minded professionals and learn from real-world case studies.

As word spread about the success of these educational initiatives, Steven's role as an industry thought-leader grew. He became a regular speaker at national conferences and a sought-after consultant for employers and advisors looking to explore self-funding for the first time. He also began working more closely with industry partners to develop innovative solutions specifically tailored to the needs of smaller employers.

One of Steven's key areas of focus has been helping brokers and advisors navigate the complex regulatory landscape around self-funding. With the passage of the Affordable Care Act and other recent healthcare reforms, the rules and requirements for self-funded plans have become increasingly complex, particularly for smaller employers. Steven has worked tirelessly to educate the industry on these changes and provide practical guidance on how to design and administer compliant plans.

Another area where Steven has made a significant impact is in the development of captive insurance programs for smaller employers. By pooling groups of similar employers in a captive arrangement, these programs allow even the smallest companies to access the benefits of self-funding while mitigating some of the volatility and risk. Steven has been a driving force behind the growth of these programs, working with top captive managers and stop-loss carriers to design and launch new products.

But perhaps the most significant contribution Steven has made to the self-insurance industry is the development of the next generation of leaders and innovators. Through his tireless efforts to educate and mentor up-and-coming professionals, he has helped to create a pipeline of talented individuals who are poised to drive the industry forward in the years ahead.

For Steven, this focus on education and professional development is more than just a personal passion—it's a strategic imperative for the entire self-insurance industry. With an aging workforce and a rapidly evolving market, he believes that investing in the next generation of talent is critical to ensuring the long-term sustainability and success of self-funding.

To that end, Steven has been a vocal advocate for expanding educational opportunities and creating new pathways for young professionals to enter the self-insurance industry. He has worked with colleges and universities to develop specialized programs in healthcare financing and risk management, and has mentored countless students and recent graduates looking to make their mark in the field.

Steven's commitment to education and mentorship has earned him a reputation as one of the most respected and admired leaders in the self-insurance industry. His peers describe him as a visionary thinker, a tireless advocate, and a true servant leader who always puts the needs of his clients and colleagues first.

As the self-insurance industry continues to evolve, Steven's influence is only going to increase. With a keen eye for emerging trends and a deep understanding of the needs of smaller employers, he is uniquely positioned to help shape the future of healthcare financing in the years ahead.

For brokers and advisors looking to succeed in this dynamic market, Steven's advice is simple but powerful: never stop learning. The self-insurance industry is constantly changing, with new products, new regulations, and new challenges emerging all the time. The most successful professionals are those who are always seeking out new knowledge, learning new skills, and who are willing to adapt in response to changing market conditions.

He also stresses the importance of building strong relationships and networks within the industry. Self-insurance is a highly collaborative business, and success often depends on the ability to partner effectively with other key stakeholders, from TPAs and stop-loss carriers to captive managers and healthcare providers. By cultivating deep relationships with these partners, brokers and advisors can unlock new opportunities and deliver better results for their clients.

Ultimately, Steven believes the key to success in the self-insurance industry is a commitment to putting clients first. Whether working with a large corporation or a small family business, the most effective professionals are those who take the time to understand their clients' unique needs, and who are willing to go the extra mile to help them achieve their goals.

It's a powerful philosophy that has guided Steven throughout his career, and one that he believes will continue to drive success in the self-insurance industry for years to come. As he looks to the future, he is excited to continue playing a role in shaping that success, and in empowering the next generation of leaders and innovators to carry the torch forward.

For those who are just starting out in the industry, Steven's message is one of encouragement and optimism. While the challenges of self-insurance can be daunting at times, he believes that the rewards—both personal and professional—are well worth the effort. With the right education, the right mindset, and the right partners, he believes that anyone can succeed in this dynamic and growing field.

So, whether you're a seasoned veteran like Steven or a newcomer just starting to explore the world of self-insurance, his advice is the same: never stop learning, never stop growing, and never lose sight of the reason you got into this business in the first place—to make a real difference in the lives of your clients and their employees. If you can do that, he believes, there's no limit to what you can achieve.

Contributor Spotlight: Ralph Weber

As the CEO of MediBid, an online marketplace that enables consumers to shop for medical services based on price and quality, Ralph Weber is on a mission to bring true market forces to bear on the healthcare industry. By empowering patients to take control of their healthcare decisions and giving providers a platform to compete for their business, he believes we can finally align incentives and drive down costs while improving outcomes.

At the heart of Ralph's vision is a belief in the power of transparency and consumerism to transform the healthcare system. For too long, he argues, patients have been kept in the dark about the true costs and quality of the care they receive, while providers have had little incentive to compete on value. The result is a system that is opaque, inefficient, and often fails to deliver the best possible outcomes for patients.

"The problem with healthcare today is that it's not really a market," Ralph explains. "Patients don't have the information they need to make informed decisions, and providers don't have the incentives to deliver high-quality, cost-effective care. It's a recipe for dysfunction."

Ralph's own journey to becoming a healthcare reformer began with a personal experience navigating the medical system. When his then wife needed surgery while they were living in Canada, they were shocked to learn that the wait time for the procedure under the country's national health system was months long, so long in fact that the wait was more than two years. Unwilling to accept such a delay, they began researching other options and ultimately decided to travel to the United States for the surgery.

What they discovered was eye-opening. Not only were they able to get the procedure done quickly at a top-notch facility, but the total cost, even paying out of pocket, was manageable. For Ralph, it was a lightbulb moment about the power of market forces to drive innovation, efficiency, and value in healthcare.

Inspired by this experience, Ralph began to study the US healthcare system in depth, looking for ways to bring more transparency and consumer choice to the market. He saw an opportunity to create an online platform that would enable patients to shop for medical services the same way they might shop for a car or a vacation—by comparing prices, reading reviews, and making informed decisions based on their own preferences and needs.

The result was MediBid, which Ralph launched in 2010 with the goal of creating a true market for healthcare services. The platform allows patients to request bids for specific procedures from a network of pre-screened providers, who compete for their business based on price and quality. Patients can compare bids side-by-side, read provider profiles and patient reviews, and ultimately choose the provider that offers the best value for their needs.

At first, the concept was met with skepticism from many in the healthcare industry. Providers pushed back against the idea of competing on price, arguing that it would lead to a "race to the bottom" and compromise quality of care. Insurers saw the platform as a threat to their business model, which relies on opaque pricing and limited consumer choice.

But Ralph persisted, believing deeply in the power of market forces to drive positive change in healthcare. He began reaching out to forward-thinking providers who saw the value in competing for patients' business and were willing to offer transparent pricing. He also worked to educate patients about their options and empower them to take a more active role in their own care.

Over time, MediBid gained traction, particularly among self-insured employers looking for ways to control costs and improve outcomes for their employees. By encouraging employees to use the platform to shop for non-emergency procedures, these employers were able to drive significant savings while still ensuring access to high-quality care.

One of the keys to MediBid's success has been its focus on quality as well as price. The platform carefully screens all providers before allowing them to bid on procedures, ensuring that they meet high standards for safety, experience, and patient satisfaction. Providers are also encouraged to post detailed profiles and patient reviews, giving consumers the information they need to make informed decisions about their care.

Another important aspect of MediBid's approach is its emphasis on direct contracting between patients and providers. By cutting out the middleman and enabling patients to contract directly with providers for their care, the platform helps to reduce administrative costs and improve price transparency. This direct contracting model also gives providers more flexibility to tailor their services to the specific needs of individual patients, rather than being constrained by one-size-fits-all insurance protocols.

As MediBid has grown, Ralph has become an increasingly vocal advocate for consumer-driven healthcare reform. He speaks frequently at conferences and events, sharing his vision for a more transparent, efficient, and patient-centered healthcare system. He has also worked to build partnerships with other organizations and stakeholders who share his commitment to driving change in the industry.

One of the most promising developments in recent years has been the growing interest in self-insured health plans among small and mid-sized employers. By combining high-deductible plans with tools like MediBid that enable employees to shop for care, these employers are able to drive down costs while still providing comprehensive coverage to their workers.

Ralph sees this trend as a major opportunity to accelerate the adoption of consumer-driven healthcare and create a more sustainable, affordable system over the long term. By empowering patients to take control of their own care and giving providers the tools and incentives to compete on value, he believes we can finally break the cycle of rising costs and declining outcomes that has plagued the industry for so long.

Looking ahead, Ralph is excited about the potential for platforms like MediBid to drive even greater transparency and competition in the healthcare market. As more patients and employers embrace the power of consumer choice, he believes we will see a wave of innovation and disruption that will ultimately lead to better care at lower costs for everyone.

At the same time, he acknowledges there are significant challenges and barriers to overcome. The healthcare industry is complex and heavily regulated, with powerful interests that are entrenched and resistant to change. Convincing patients to take a more active role in their own care can also be an uphill battle, particularly for those who are used to the traditional, paternalistic model of medicine.

But Ralph remains optimistic that the tide is turning, and that the forces of consumerism and transparency will ultimately prevail. As more patients, providers, and payers see the benefits of a market-driven approach to healthcare, he believes the momentum for change will become unstoppable.

For those on the front lines of this transformation, Ralph has some advice: "Stay focused on the patient," he urges. "At the end of the day, that's who this is all about—giving patients the tools and information they need to make the best possible decisions about their own care. If we can do that, everything else will fall into place."

He also stresses the importance of building collaborative relationships with other stakeholders in the industry, from providers and payers to policymakers and patient advocates. "No one can do this alone," he notes. "We need to work together to create a system that puts patients first and aligns everyone's incentives around delivering the best possible care at the most affordable price."

Ultimately, Ralph believes that the transformation of healthcare will require a fundamental shift in mindset—away from the old model of medicine and toward a new, patient-centered approach that empowers individuals to take control of their health and wellbeing. It's a shift that won't happen overnight, but one that he believes is inevitable as market forces continue to shape the industry.

"The future of healthcare is consumer-driven," Ralph asserts. "And while there will certainly be bumps in the road, I'm confident that we're heading in the right direction. By putting patients first and harnessing the power of transparency and competition, we can create a system that delivers better care, better outcomes, and better value for everyone."

It's a vision that has driven Ralph Weber throughout his career, and one that continues to inspire his work at MediBid every day. And while the journey is far from over, he knows that every bid placed, every price compared, and every patient empowered is another step toward a brighter, healthier future for us all.

WHAT THEY SEE AND DON'T SEE

"Is your no a no or a not yet?"
   — *An Unknown Supplicant to God*

In the competitive world of health insurance, every seasoned broker has faced rejection at some point. Prospects who initially seem interested suddenly go cold, leaving the broker wondering what went wrong. But these "no's" aren't always the dead ends they appear to be. With the right approach, it's possible to transform many of these rejections into enthusiastic "yes's" that become the backbone of your book of business.

When I first pitched Joe on the benefits of Level Funding, he was skeptical of any alternative funding arrangements. He was the owner of a small auto parts distribution company, and he had been burned by skyrocketing premiums under his fully-insured plan. When I emphasized the potential for savings and surplus refunds via a self-funded plan, he quickly shut me down.

"Look, I've heard it all before," he said. "Every year, some new broker comes in here promising to save me money, and every year my rates still go up. I'm tired of the run-around. I just need a simple, predictable plan for my employees, not some complicated scheme. Thanks, but no thanks."

Deflated, I retreated to my office, wondering where I went wrong. Joe seemed like the perfect candidate for Level Funding—a small business owner struggling with double-digit rate hikes and desperate for relief. What had I missed?

As I reviewed my notes from the meeting, a realization dawned on me. In my eagerness to evangelize the virtues of Level Funding, I had neglected Joe's concerns. I was so focused on touting the potential rewards that I glossed over the complexities he would have to navigate as an employer. No wonder he saw my proposal as just another empty promise.

Armed with this insight, I decided to take a different tack. Instead of another hard sell on Level Funding, I reached back out to Joe with a simple request—to learn more about his business and the challenges he faced. I made it clear that I wasn't looking to pitch him anything, but rather to listen and understand.

Joe agreed to meet for coffee. Over the course of an hour, he opened up about the pressures of running a small business. He shared his frustrations with the opaque, convoluted world of health insurance and his fear of exposing his company to unknown financial risks. Above all, he expressed his deep desire to care for his loyal employees while staying afloat.

As I listened, I realized that Joe's initial "no" to Level Funding wasn't a rejection of the concept itself, but rather a reflection of his underlying anxieties and unmet needs. He didn't need a slick sales pitch, but an empathetic advisor who could guide him through the intricacies of self-funding with patience, clarity, and total transparency.

So that's exactly what I set out to become. Over the following weeks, I worked closely with Joe to explore if Level Funding was even a good fit for him. We went through detailed claims projections and I outlined the specific stop-loss protections that would limit his exposure.

Slowly but surely, Joe's skepticism melted away and was replaced by a cautious optimism. He began to see Level Funding not as a leap into the unknown, but as an opportunity to take control of his health insurance spend while still protecting his bottom line. And when I presented him with a comprehensive proposal showing how he could save 15% on his current spend while simultaneously enhancing his employees' coverage, he was ready to take the plunge.

That initial "no" from Joe wasn't a failure on my part, but rather an opportunity to deepen my understanding of his needs and craft a more compelling solution. By taking the time to listen, educate, and build trust, I was able to transform a hard "no" into an enthusiastic "yes" that blossomed into a long-term partnership.

Over the years, I've honed this consultative approach into a repeatable process. Here are some key principles I've learned:

- **Listen more than you speak.** When a prospect tells you "no," resist the urge to jump into rebuttal mode. Instead, get curious about the root causes behind their objections. Ask open-ended questions to surface their underlying fears, frustrations, and desired outcomes. The better you understand their world, the more effectively you can tailor your pitch.
- **Lead with empathy, not ego.** It's easy to take rejection personally, especially when you believe passionately in your solution. But remember, it's not about you. Put yourself in the prospect's shoes and acknowledge the validity of their concerns. Show that you're on their side, not just out to make a quick buck.
- **Educate, don't manipulate.** Nobody likes feeling pressured or backed into a corner. Rather than hammering prospects with high-octane closes, focus on empowering

them with the knowledge they need to make an informed decision. Break down complex concepts into relatable terms, provide clear examples and case studies, and give them space to digest and reflect.

- **Build a bulletproof business case.** Overcoming a "no" often comes down to demonstrating irrefutable value. Take the time to thoroughly understand the prospect's current state and quantify the hard and soft costs of inaction. Then, build a detailed business case showing how your solution can measurably improve their bottom line while mitigating risk. Numbers don't lie.

- **Offer a clear path forward.** Converting a "no" into a "yes" is only half the battle. To seal the deal, you need to paint a vivid picture of what success looks like and how you'll get there together. Map out a clear onboarding plan with milestones and deliverables. The more confident prospects feel in your ability to execute, the more likely they are to take the leap.

- **Stay persistent.** Just because a prospect tells you "no" once doesn't mean the game is over. Continue to check in periodically with valuable insights and updates, always leading with a service mindset. You never know when a trigger event like a big rate hike or a key employee health issue will reopen the door. By staying top of mind and consistently adding value, you'll be the first person they call when they're finally ready to say "yes."

Of course, some "no's" are non-negotiable, and it's important to discern when to respectfully move on. But in my experience, a surprising number of initial rejections can be flipped with the right mix of empathy, education, and persistence. The key is to view every "no" not as a personal failure, but as an invitation to learn, adapt, and come back with an even more compelling solution.

I remember one particularly challenging case in my career that perfectly illustrates this principle. The prospect, a mid-sized restaurant chain, had been burned by self-funding in the past and had sworn off any form of alternative risk financing for good. When I initially reached out to pitch my services, the CFO practically laughed me out of the room.

"We tried the whole self-funding thing a few years back," he scoffed, "and it was an unmitigated disaster. Claims far exceeded projections, we blew through our reserve fund and had a massive deficit."

Rather than trying to convince him he was wrong, I leaned in with curiosity. "That sounds incredibly stressful," I said. "I'm so sorry you had to go through that. Would you be open to sharing more about what went sideways? I'd love to understand how we could avoid a repeat scenario."

Taken aback by my non-defensive response, the CFO walked me through the gory details. It quickly became apparent that their former broker had severely underestimated the risk profile of their population. There was a high rate of smoking and obesity among their employees, and their workforce lacked training on safety protocols. None of this was accounted for in the company's prior self-funded plan.

Armed with that context, I was able to reframe the conversation around how a properly structured level funded plan with adequate stop loss protection and integrated cost containment measures could deliver the predictability they craved while still unlocking savings. I introduced them to my elite underwriting team and proposed a thorough health risk assessment to ensure we had a crystal clear picture of their exposures. And I mapped out a multi-year roadmap showing how we could use data-driven insights to bend their cost curve over time without compromising care quality.

By leading with empathy, taking the time to deeply understand their past pain, and positioning Level Funding as the antidote to their prior nightmare, I was able to gradually chip away at their resistance. It took multiple meetings and a whole lot of hand-holding, but eventually they agreed to give self-funding another shot—this time with the right safeguards and support in place.

Objections, even the most vehement ones, are often just disguised cries for help. By approaching them with compassion, curiosity, and a relentless commitment to problem-solving, you can transform even the biggest skeptics into your biggest advocates.

Of course, this is often easier said than done, especially when you're first starting out and feeling the pressure to quickly build a book of business. It's tempting to adopt a "quick no is better than a slow maybe" mentality and move on to the next prospect at the first sign of resistance. But trust me when I say that learning to embrace the "no" and lean into those tough conversations is one of the most valuable skills you can develop as a benefits advisor.

CLIENT RETENTION THROUGH PROACTIVE ENGAGEMENT

"People don't care how much you know until they know how much you care."
— Theodore Roosevelt

Amidst the many challenges facing young health insurance agents building their book of business through Level Funding—from fraud, waste, and abuse, to aggressive competitors—perhaps the most important thing you can do to survive and thrive long-term is to proactively engage with your existing groups. Retaining loyal clients is always more profitable and efficient than racing to replace lost accounts. The key lies in staying one step ahead of issues before they flare up into relationship-straining crises.

I learned this lesson the hard way after nearly losing one of my first

Level Funded groups, a mid-sized auto repair shop. We had transitioned them to a self-funded plan the year prior and they were on track to receive a sizable surplus fund. I thought everything was going smoothly, so I shifted my focus to bringing in new business. I figured no news was good news from the client.

To my shock, just a few months before their renewal date, I received a terse email from the owner stating they had made the decision to return to their old, fully-insured carrier and would not need my services any further. Blindsided and bewildered, I reached out to request an emergency meeting. Sitting across the conference table from the grim-faced owner and CFO, I asked what had gone wrong. Hadn't the plan performed well with utilization running below expected? Weren't they positioned to get a significant chunk of money back in a surplus check? Why on earth would they want to abandon the Level Funded approach just as it was about to pay off?

The owner sighed. "Tom, the plan design itself has been fine. We've had no major issues with employee access to care or provider pushback. But the day-to-day administration of the plan has been a nightmare. My HR manager is drowning in employee questions and complaints about the claims process. I've sent you several emails that have gone unanswered. Frankly, we're tired of feeling like we've been left to fend for ourselves. So, we've decided to simplify our lives and go back to the fully-insured model, even if it costs us more."

In that moment, it all clicked. It wasn't some sneaky competitor or plan design flaw that was threatening to unravel this account—it was my own complacency and lack of proactive engagement. Wrapped up in the adrenaline rush of new sales, I had neglected the blocking and tackling of daily account management. Of course the client felt abandoned and wanted to bail—I had made myself scarce after the close instead of rolling up my sleeves to ensure smooth implementation.

Chastened but determined, I owned up to dropping the ball and begged for a chance to make things right. I promised to immediately escalate their service issues and to schedule bi-weekly touch base calls to stay on top of any brewing concerns. Moreover, I committed to quarterly stewardship reviews to assess plan performance, identify cost containment opportunities, and explore any benefit enhancements made possible by accrued surplus. To demonstrate that I meant business, I blocked off my calendar that very afternoon and camped out in the shop's break room, buying pizza for the staff and personally fielding their questions about the claims submission process.

By the end of the day, the owner agreed to give me one more shot to turn the experience around before making a final decision on renewal. Over the next three months, I practically embedded myself with the client. I met with the HR manager weekly to review employee issues and provide additional education on how to utilize the plan. I monitored their claims data like a hawk, proactively reaching out at the first sign of any adverse utilization trends. When an employee had a baby three months premature requiring NICU care that threatened to pierce the aggregate stop loss attachment point, I was on the phone that same day to invoke a HIPAA-compliant large case management program to ensure both optimal treatment and judicious use of plan assets.

By the time renewal rolled around, the auto shop's attitude toward their level funded plan had completely turned around. Not only did they opt to stay the course, but the owner went out of his way to express how impressed he was with my newfound attentiveness and willingness to go the extra mile. That retention preserved over $70,000 in annualized revenue for me—money that would have walked out the door had I remained complacent.

I share this story not to boast, but to illustrate just how critical proactive client engagement is when it comes to thriving as a Level Funding broker. It's not enough to set it and forget it. You have to stay actively involved, continuously demonstrating your value and heading off problems before they metastasize. Here are some best practices I've learned over the years for retaining level funded groups through proactive engagement:

- **Schedule regular check-in calls:** Don't wait for the client to reach out with issues. Set recurring touch-points to proactively assess their experience and nip any festering problems in the bud. The goal is to make them feel like you're an extension of their HR/Finance team.
- **Monitor claims data religiously:** Don't just rely on the TPA or carrier to alert you to adverse plan performance. Insist on receiving regular claims reporting and learn how to quickly identify worrisome utilization trends. The earlier you intervene with targeted participant outreach and education, the better the odds of getting things back on track.
- **Conduct formal stewardship reviews:** At least once a quarter, sit down with the key decision-makers to review high-level plan metrics, assess progress toward clinical and financial goals, and chart out upcoming priorities. This demonstrates your strategic value while surfacing any festering frustrations.
- **Provide concierge-level service:** Position yourself as the client's health plan ombudsman, advocating tirelessly on their behalf with the numerous vendors involved in delivering the benefit. When complications arise, as they inevitably will, be the first to jump on the problem and own it through to resolution instead of finger pointing.
- **Continuously educate and advise:** An informed client is an engaged client. The more they understand the inner workings of their plan and how their employees' healthcare consumption behaviors drive financial performance, the more committed they'll be to self-funding over time. Make it your mission to demystify the complexities and empower better decisions.
- **Celebrate the wins together:** When those surplus checks come in, hand deliver them with much pomp and

circumstance. Remind the client that this surplus is only made possible through their prudent plan management coupled with your expert guidance. Position it as a shared win worth toasting to incentivize continued partnership.

- **Solicit feedback constantly:** Don't assume you know how the client is feeling. Seek out frequent input on what's working well, what could work better, and how you can improve your service delivery. Demonstrating genuine humility and openness to constructive criticism builds trust and loyalty.

- **Leverage your centers of influence:** Foster close working relationships with your key client contacts at the TPA and carrier. Be able to call in favors when needed to get fast resolutions and white glove treatment. The more you're seen going to bat behind the scenes, the more valued you'll be.

- **Never get complacent:** The second you start taking a client's business for granted is the second you open the door to getting displaced. No matter how well the plan is running, maintain a healthy sense of paranoia and relentlessly look for ways to defend your incumbent position.

Admittedly, this approach to client engagement is more time intensive than the traditional fully-insured model. You can't just sell the plan, set it, and forget it. Level funded plans require continuous care. But that's also their greatest competitive advantage—once you demonstrate your unparalleled ability to quarterback the moving pieces, you become difficult to dislodge. Your clients will see you not as some nameless, faceless peddler of policies, but as an indispensable strategic partner.

Of course, devoting such personalized attention to every client is only feasible if you're disciplined about the type of business you write.

If you're constantly chasing after every small group in your market, you'll inevitably end up spread too thin, and your service will suffer. That's why it's so critical to hone in on your ideal niche of Level Funding ready prospects and cultivate deep expertise in catering to their unique needs. Better to go an inch wide and a mile deep than to be a jack of all trades, master of none.

It's also important to recognize that not every client will be receptive to such high-touch engagement—some will always prefer a more transactional approach. You have to pick your battles and focus your energy on those accounts that demonstrate a willingness to collaborate as true partners in the Level Funding journey. Over time, you'll develop a sixth sense for which clients are worth spending the extra effort to retain versus those that will never fully appreciate your value-add to their business.

After all, being a great salesperson will only take you so far in this business. To thrive as a Level Funding broker, you have to be an even better service provider. That means embedding yourself with your clients, anticipating their needs, and moving heaven and earth to exceed their expectations. It's not sexy work, but it's the only way to build a book of business that can withstand the slings and arrows of a hyper-competitive marketplace.

Overcoming Skepticism: Educating Clients on Benefits

"Formal education will make you a living. Self-education will make you a fortune."
—*Jim Rohn*

A major challenge in selling Level-Funded health plans is overcoming the skepticism many employers (and brokers) initially feel about unfamiliar concepts like self-insurance and stop loss policies. Carefully educating prospects on the concrete benefits of Level Funding is key to convincing them that Level Funding is a true win-win.

I learned an early lesson when I attempted to convert brokers who were selling traditional models to selling Level-Funded plans instead. Initially, I thought the cost-saving potential and adaptability of these plans would be self-evident. But I soon discovered that even the most experienced brokers viewed these plans as too unconventional for their small business clients.

One broker shared, "I've been with Big Carrier for two decades. Every company on Main Street relies on it. Convincing them to leave a functioning system for an untried self-funded plan is tough. I'd rather keep things as they are."

Many agents were hesitant. They saw Level Funding as a risky proposition, packed with intricate rules that could offset any potential benefits. They feared their clients might struggle to comprehend the complexities of this plan. And they were also afraid of any potential issues that could damage their reputation. Simply put, unfamiliar territory sparked a sense of fear that made them overlook it.

If you're a broker who's unsure about using the Level Funding model independently, don't worry. Our company can join forces with you, offering the knowledge needed to develop plans for optimal returns. We can guide you through particulars such as stop-loss agreements, reference-based pricing, and determining reserve targets. If you wish to maintain your existing client relationships while also benefiting from the capabilities of Level Funding, we can arrange a general agent introduction.

In talking with brokers, I found that a few key doubts kept them tied to traditional insurance plans, even as these plans became more expensive and less flexible. I addressed these doubts with clear, persuasive arguments that made sense both logically and emotionally. Once brokers felt truly heard, they were more open to rethinking their existing beliefs. And these doubts are the same obstacles you can expect to face when talking to potential clients. So, what are these doubts?

The first hurdle I encountered was skepticism. It was hard for brokers to believe that self-funded plans might lead to surplus funds of massive sums. They were convinced that businesses would need a high level of self-control to prevent activating their stop-loss protections, which could deplete any surplus. In short, it seemed too good to be true.

When discussing Level Funding, patience and clarity are crucial. It's helpful to explain how it works in detail. Show skeptics a range of possible outcomes, good and bad, based on a company's risk profile. Talk about the break-even point and potential surplus funds at different usage levels. Compare this to expected premium increases for similar corporate plans. Your underwriting expertise can support your explanation and help them understand the process.

The second obstacle I faced was self-doubt. Many brokers tend to avoid the concept of self-insurance and stop-loss arrangements due to their perceived complexity. They fear that it might introduce instability or compliance issues, especially for clients new to the field. Explaining these concepts can seem overwhelming, given their strict compliance requirements. As a result, brokers often stick with traditional corporate policies, avoiding discussions about their possible limitations or conflicts.

To address concerns around perceived complexity, clear and informative sessions with absolute transparency are key. Assure potential clients that you will help manage the intricate tasks, such as filing and paperwork. Supply comprehensive guides comparing Level Funding to alternate strategies in the event situations change. Highlight the benefits and drawbacks, like improved control and better management of cash flow. And address potential risks head-on. This strategy will enable your clients to feel secure, enabling them to recommend the most suitable plans.

I also found that some brokers view Level Funding as a risky path with minor savings that could backfire dramatically. They believe that traditional insurance providers offer more stability, even if it means giving up potential profits to minimize risk. In essence, they choose the 'better safe than sorry' approach, valuing job security over innovative strategies. Not surprisingly, many would-be clients feel the same way.

When first introduced to Level Funding, most people find the model to be so novel that they inherently don't trust it...even though companies like mine have been successfully implementing it for decades. Still, their feelings are valid and must be addressed. In such a situation, your role is to subtly challenge these preconceived notions while being mindful of their concerns. Highlight the fact that even traditional business policies could change when renewal time comes. Clearly demonstrate cost trends over a span of 3-5 years, taking into account medical inflation. Discuss the client's goals beyond merely reducing premium costs in the initial year. Gradually steer the conversation from avoiding dangers toward aligning plans with long-term objectives.

The largest hurdle to overcome is personal pride, especially for veteran brokers who might find it challenging to adopt new approaches after years of unaltered success. Pointing out these flaws can often lead to defensiveness and further entrench their beliefs. However, when you introduce Level Funding as a natural progression in their existing workflow, it's seen as evolution rather than revolution.

Reducing prideful contrarianism in employers often involves debunking myths that fuel resistance to change. Potential clients who are open to learning see this process as an opportunity to deepen their market knowledge, not as a challenge to their competence. The secret to helping those who are resistant to change lies in understanding that their hesitation typically arises from fear, rather than stubbornness or lack of skill. By understanding your clients, addressing their main concerns, and supporting them at their pace, you become a more effective guide.

When people face major changes that can affect their daily lives, they often have doubts and need reassurance. In these situations, empathy is key. Responding with understanding to their fear of risk can build trust. This bond can significantly reduce tension and allow them to reconsider their existing views.

Data serves as a compelling instrument to convince skeptics, too. Showcasing high client retention rates over multiple years indicates ongoing satisfaction, not just initial enthusiasm. Offering industry benchmarks for claim accuracy can negate the notion that accurate underwriting is limited to large groups. Dispelling fears based on misunderstandings is easier when you present solid facts about risk controls and safety measures.

One practical way to address doubts is by hosting small, informal seminars with other brokers who once had doubts themselves. Away from the pressure of high-stakes sales, these relaxed meetups allow executives to openly discuss Level-Funded plans. The ambiance puts attendees at ease and provides a place for them to share their challenges with corporate renewals. This honest exchange fosters a sense of unity and partnership, reinforcing the idea that brokers and carriers both share a commitment to resolving issues.

The small business consulting industry can sometimes feel complex and unwelcoming. That's why unity is crucial. It encourages growth and reduces uncertainties. I introduce Level Funding as a simple, grass-roots innovation, not as a top-down directive. This approach often changes the minds of those initially resistant to the idea, turning them from stubborn defenders of the old ways into curious explorers.

The perks of Level Funding might not be clear at first glance. But when explained well, any doubts tend to fade, replaced by a keen interest sparked by understanding. Those who grasp it early on become ardent advocates, spreading the word about their newly discovered knowledge.

I recall a chat with a previous skeptic. "At first, I thought this was all trickery," he confessed. "But now, I see how detailed underwriting can make these plans work, even for small employers. Seeing a substantial surplus certainly changed my mind!"

Rather than getting into direct conflicts with staunch traditionalists, softly challenging their misconceptions can gradually reduce resistance against innovation. Keep in mind, a well-executed argument can persuade people more convincingly than an outright battle. Before highlighting the potential paybacks from Level Funding, it's vital to clear up any lingering misconceptions about the power of innovation.

When fear subsides and understanding takes root, acceptance naturally follows. When trusted peers become supporters, they provide the social validation needed to inspire broader acceptance. As pioneering patients adapt, others tend to follow their lead. However, it's crucial to address fears by demonstrating understanding, not just spewing statistics.

With the confidence gained from understanding, we can create an environment where it's safe to question and explore. These spaces are crucial for sparking curiosity and fostering a culture of learning and innovation. When people feel safe in their ignorance, they're more likely to take risks, ask questions, and discover new ways of thinking. Encouragement and patience in this process are crucial. Remember, not everyone will embrace change at the same pace, and that's okay.

Fraud, Uncovered Claims, & Kamikazes

"Fraud, waste and abuse violate the brother rule."
— Unknown

The waters of any career do not always provide smooth sailing, and health insurance brokers are no exception. There are countless ways selling Level-Funded plans can go wrong, but most problems can be placed in three categories. For each category of problems, there are common-sense strategies you can take to hedge your troubles. Consider this chapter advice for your career's preventative care.

The four categories of problems you will face are as follows:

1. Fraud, waste, and abuse
2. Uncovered claims
3. Kamikaze competitors

This chapter isn't meant to scare you, but you want to know what you don't know. Early mistakes can have a compounding effect on the security of your career. The sooner you can get a grip on these problems, the sooner you can build a stable book of business that will last you a lifetime. So, let's get into it. First up, fraud, waste, and abuse.

WILLFUL OMISSIONS, NONDISCLOSURES, AND INTENTIONAL DECEPTION

"You can build a throne of bayonets, but you can't sit on it for long."
— *Boris Yeltsin*

As a young insurance agent building your book of business through Level Funding, you'll need to be prepared to navigate some treacherous waters. One of the biggest challenges you're likely to face is clients who intentionally withhold information or fail to disclose key details that impact the risk profile and underwriting of their plan. This can range from "forgetting" to mention an employee's serious preexisting condition, to willful omissions, nondisclosures, and intentional deception like signing up a family member as an employee who doesn't actually work for the company.

I encountered a painful example of this with a small marketing agency. The owner, let's call her Janet (not her real name), was eager to sign up for a Level-Funded plan. She assured me her 15 employees were all in good health with no major issues. We went through the underwriting process and everything checked out, so we got them approved and launched the plan.

Three months later, I received a call from my claims department: *"We have a problem."* A man listed as an employee of Janet's company was diagnosed with late stage renal cancer and was set to begin an expensive treatment regimen. His medical expenses were going to blow way past the amount we had set aside in claims funding for this group.

When I looked into it further, I discovered this man was actually Janet's uncle. He didn't work at the marketing agency at all. I called Janet and confronted her about the situation. At first she played dumb, acting like it must have been some sort of clerical error. But when I pressed her on it, she finally admitted that she had added her sick uncle to the plan without telling me.

"I didn't think it would be a big deal," she said, "I was just trying to help my family. I didn't realize how expensive his treatment would be."

Janet's decision put me in a terrible position. By failing to disclose the truth about her uncle's health and employment status, she had intentionally deceived the carrier. I had no choice but to cancel her policy and even report the incident to the proper authorities. It was a hard lesson learned about how one person's intentional deception can jeopardize an entire plan.

As unfair as it might seem to you as the agent in a situation like this, the reality is that in the eyes of the stop loss carrier backing the plan, the liability for these kinds of omissions and nondisclosures falls on your shoulders. You're the one who has to deal with the fallout and rebuild trust with the underwriters. That's why it is so critical that you do your own due diligence during the underwriting process to sniff out any potential issues. Don't just take the group's word that everything is on the up and up.

Some common red flags I've learned to watch out for over the years include:

- Employees with the same last name as the owner who were recently added to the census
- Employees who seem to have an unusually large number of dependents on the plan

- Any employee or dependent with an address far outside the company's geographic area
- Prescriptions for high cost specialty drugs showing up on an employee's pharmacy history that don't match their stated medical conditions
- Hesitation or pushback from any employee when you ask for details about medical history during underwriting

If the business owner makes you uneasy, your gut is probably telling you something.

Dig into it. Ask for documentation like tax returns or pay stubs to verify an employee's status. Compare the group's census month over month to see if any new employees were suddenly added right before you started the underwriting process. Cross reference pharmacy records against doctor visits and hospital stays. You might feel like you're being too nosy or invasive. But I assure you this is not an area where you can afford to cut corners or give someone the benefit of the doubt. If you end up with even one big undisclosed claimant, it can torpedo the whole program, jack up future renewals, and damage your credibility with underwriters and other clients.

There are also some groups that intentionally leave unhealthy employees off the census completely. They think they're gaming the system by having their youngest, healthiest employees on the Level-Funded plan to keep claims low while secretly keeping their older, sicker employees on a separate fully insured plan. That's called "carving out" and it's a big no-no. It's your job to make sure you have a complete census of the company and that all eligible employees are either enrolling in the plan or signing a waiver. No exceptions.

As a third party administrator, my team does much of this detective work on behalf of our broker partners. We have an in-house underwriting unit that conducts deep dives into each group—running background checks, prescription histories, and medical records through various databases to search for any undisclosed risk factors. It's a painstaking process, but we see it as a critical part of our role in making Level Funding successful for all parties.

Still, there are steps you can take as a broker to protect yourself and your clients. Insist on getting a signed disclosure form from every employee during the underwriting process attesting that they have provided complete and accurate information. Have the owner sign off on the final census and plan design to confirm that nothing has been left off. Include language in your client agreement that puts the onus on them to be forthright and gives you the right to terminate the contract if intentional deceptions or misrepresentations are discovered.

The vast majority of clients have no intention of deceiving you. But there will always be a few bad apples who see Level Funding as an opportunity to get one over the system. It's on you to disabuse them of that notion and make the consequences of nondisclosure abundantly clear. A little healthy fear of cheating is no bad thing in business.

At the end of the day, you have to be willing to walk away from a case if something doesn't smell right, even if it means giving up a potentially big commission. Your reputation is worth more than any single sale. If word gets around that you're not running a tight ship, you'll have a hard time placing cases and growing your business. But if you thoroughly vet your groups and keep a watchful eye out for fraud, waste, and abuse, you'll develop a stellar track record that opens doors.

Being an insurance agent requires putting on a lot of different hats —salesperson, consultant, analyst, educator, relationship manager. But when it comes to sniffing out fraud, waste, and abuse, you need to channel your inner detective. Develop a keen eye for spotting things that don't quite add up. Ask probing questions and demand documentation where needed. And always trust your gut.

By sharpening your skills at navigating around these potential land mines, you'll be able to steer your clients toward plans that don't blow up in their faces. You'll build a book of sustainable business rather than a house of cards waiting to collapse at the first stiff breeze. Amidst the competitive pressures, staying true to your integrity is what will set you apart in the long run.

Claims Outside of the Traditional Window

"If it smells too good to be true, it probably is."
— Unknown

Even if you thoroughly vet your groups and keep a watchful eye out for fraud, waste, and abuse, that doesn't mean you're completely out of the woods once a Level-Funded plan is up and running. One of the other big challenges that can broadside you as a broker is claims that come in outside of the policy's active coverage window.

Let me give you an example. I once took on a small auto parts distributor with about 20 employees. The owner, Joe, was a straight shooter and very transparent throughout the underwriting process. We got them approved and they had a pretty uneventful first plan year from a claims perspective. No big losses and no major issues. We ended up renewing them for a second year with a nominal increase and called it a day.

Then, just as their second plan year was wrapping up, I got a call from the claims department that they had received a hospital bill for one of Joe's employees to the tune of $180,000. This wasn't a new claim, though. The date of service on the bill was a full 14 months prior, smack dab in the middle of their first plan year.

Apparently the employee, who had since been terminated, was in a nasty car accident and received treatment at an out of network trauma center. But for some reason, the hospital didn't get around to submitting the claim until over a year later. We were in a pickle. The bill was legit—the charges were valid and the employee was covered at the time of service. But the plan had what's called a 12/18 contract on it, meaning the group only has coverage for claims incurred within the 12 month policy period and paid within 18 months. This is pretty standard for most small-group self-funded plans. And it meant the stop loss carrier wasn't obligated to pay for claims submitted this late.

With the group now in a new plan year with a new stop loss contract, the old policy had essentially evaporated. As a broker, you walk a tightrope in these scenarios. On one hand, you want to be a strong advocate for your client. You want to go to bat for them with the stop loss carrier or TPA to see if there's any way to make an exception or find wiggle room to pay the claim. You don't want to just roll over and stick your client with a huge, unexpected bill if you can help it.

But on the other hand, you have to abide by the plan document and the agreement that was signed. If you bend the rules or try to force the issue, you can damage your credibility or put yourself in an errors and omissions bind. In my case with Joe, I got lucky. I explained to him that even though his former-employee's claim occurred during a period when he was covered, we had no mechanism for paying it now that the plan year had closed. Joe, to my surprise, took the news like a champ. He understood that it wasn't anything nefarious on our part. But he was still on the hook for this massive bill that had just materialized out of thin air.

We ended up working out a deal where the plan would pay a portion of it and Joe's company would cover the rest. It was a bitter pill to swallow. Thankfully, there are some safeguards you can put in place to protect against these late claims. You can negotiate with the stop loss carrier to have a longer run-out period for claims submission—say a 12/24 contract that gives an extra 12 months for providers to get their billing ducks in a row. You can also work with your TPA to be more proactive about chasing down claims and following up with providers throughout the plan year, rather than just waiting for them to come in on their own.

But ultimately, no system is perfect. The reality is that in this business, you're always going to have to contend with a certain degree of claims volatility. Providers are notoriously terrible at timely filing. You might have some hospitals that are on top of it and submit claims within a week of discharge. Others might sit on them for months and then suddenly vomit out a whole stack at once. Some may even try to game the system by holding claims until the next plan year to avoid aggregating against the current stop loss deductible. It's maddening.

Your best defense is to educate your clients and manage their expectations. Have frank conversations with them about late claim submission risk during the sales process. Explain that while Level Funding can be a great tool for controlling costs, it's not a silver bullet. There's always the potential for Murphy's Law to rear its ugly head. Encourage them to build up a claims reserve surplus in the early years so they have a cushion if and when that big, ugly bill shows up down the road.

As the broker, it's also critical that you stay on top of your client's claims throughout the plan year. Don't just set up the plan and forget it. Keep in close contact with your TPA and review claims data at least quarterly to spot any troubling utilization trends early on. If you see that a group is running way ahead of projections mid-year, sound the alarm bells and work with them to implement cost containment measures rather than just hoping things will magically get better. The further ahead of problems you can get, the more options you'll have to course correct.

THE THREAT OF KAMIKAZE COMPETITORS

"The storm whispers, 'You cannot withstand me.' The warrior responds, 'I am the storm.'"
— Unknown

As a broker helping small business clients enjoy the benefits of Level-Funded health plans, you must remain vigilant against encroachment from agents still stuck in the fully-insured mindset. These "kamikaze" competitors may attempt to undermine your hard work by swooping in and offering temporarily lower rates to steal away your groups, especially right before you're about to deliver a surplus check.

I face this tactic constantly and it can be frustrating, especially after putting in months of work to transition a company over to a Level-Funded plan. I worked with one small manufacturing company that had just wrapped up their first plan year, and was on track to deliver a sizable surplus. But right before I could break the good news, the owner called.

"Tom, I just got off the phone with a broker from one of the big national carriers. They quoted us rates for next year that are 20% lower than what we paid this year with you. I thought you said this self-funded approach was supposed to save us money? What's going on?"

My heart sank. I knew exactly what was happening. This client had become a prime target for predatory agents looking to pad their numbers. They saw that we had put in the hard work to get the company running efficiently on a Level-Funded plan, and now they wanted to swoop in and reap the rewards by offering an artificially low renewal rate.

I asked the owner to send me over the proposal so I could analyze it. Sure enough, it was rife with red flags. The medical underwriting was paper thin and completely ignored the group's actual claims experience. The rates were based on a "community rating" that lumped them in with other small groups, healthy and unhealthy alike. And the network discounts were paltry compared to what we had negotiated. In all likelihood, the company would pay a 20% discount on their first year only to receive a 30% increase the next year...and then again the year after that.

I called the owner back and walked him through my concerns. I explained how the fully-insured approach incentivizes carriers to lowball rates in the first year only to jack them up in future renewals once the group is locked in. I cautioned that while the initial 20% savings might look appealing, it could quickly evaporate and then some. Most importantly, I pointed out that by switching to this plan, he would be forfeiting the $35,000 surplus his company was on pace to receive in just a few short months.

To his credit, the owner listened intently and asked thoughtful questions. He admitted that he had been dazzled by the big rate decrease and hadn't scrutinized the fine print. He agreed that abandoning the Level-Funded strategy just as it was about to bear fruit would be short-sighted. And he expressed appreciation that I took the time to educate him rather than just badmouthing the competitor.

In the end, the client stuck with our Level-Funded plan and reaped the rewards. But it was a wake up call for me about the lengths some agents will go to steal business. It's not enough to just structure a great plan for your clients. You have to be proactive about defending it. Here are some lessons I've learned over the years about protecting your groups from kamikaze competitors:

- **Stay in constant communication.** Don't just reach out to your clients at renewal time. Check in with them throughout the year to see how things are going, and provide updates on their claims utilization. The more face time you have, the harder it will be for another agent to swoop in and get a one-off conversion.

- **Educate early and often.** Make sure your clients understand how Level Funding works and what makes it different from fully-insured plans. Arm them with data on how their plan is performing and how surplus funds are calculated. The more informed they are, the less likely they'll be swayed by shallow promises.

- **Sell the long-term vision.** Emphasize that you're not just focused on getting them the lowest rates for the coming plan year. You're invested in being their strategic partner for years to come. Show them projections of their savings over a 3-5 year period and how those savings can be reinvested into their business.
- **Call out questionable practices.** If you catch wind of a competitor quoting rates that seem too good to be true, don't be afraid to dig into the details and expose any smoke and mirrors. Highlight where they may be cutting corners or glossing over important caveats. Your clients deserve to know the truth.
- **Get everything in writing.** Insist that any competitive quotes shared with your clients are submitted in writing so you can do a thorough apples-to-apples comparison. If an agent is being intentionally vague or evasive, that's a red flag.
- **Leverage your partnerships.** If you're working with a reputable TPA or stop-loss carrier, lean on them for support when fending off competitors. They have a vested interest in client retention too, and may be able to provide additional ammo like network analyses or case studies to bolster your defense.
- **Be willing to walk away.** No matter how much you like a client or how big the account is, there may come a point where it's not worth fighting tooth and nail to keep their business if they refuse to see reason. Wish them well and move on gracefully. Chances are they'll learn their lesson the hard way and come knocking on your door again in a year or two.

Losing a client to a kamikaze competitor after doing all the heavy lifting is a gut punch that every broker experiences at some point. It can make you question your value and your place in the industry. But remember, you can't control the actions of others, only your response to them.

By staying focused on being an indispensable advisor to your clients and always taking the high road, you'll build a loyal book of business that can weather any short-term poaching attempts. You'll develop a reputation as a trusted partner rather than just another vendor. And when those wayward clients do eventually come back to you, as they so often do, resist the urge to say "I told you so." Welcome them back with open arms and get to work on giving them the guidance they should have heeded in the first place.

Outmaneuvering kamikaze competitors is not about fighting fire with fire or sinking to their level. It's about rising above the fray and demonstrating through your actions what it means to be a true proponent of your clients' success. If you do that consistently, you'll win far more business than you'll ever lose.

As I reflect back on my own journey in this business, I'm struck by how much my perspective has evolved. When I first started out, I thought being a successful broker was all about hustling hard and closing deals. But over time, I've come to realize that true success is measured not just by the size of your commission checks, but by the depth of your client relationships and the positive impact you have on their lives.

That's why I'm passionate about ethical competition in our industry. Because when brokers compete on the basis of integrity, expertise, and client service, everyone wins. Small businesses get access to affordable, high-quality health coverage. Employees and their families enjoy better health outcomes. And brokers build thriving practices based on trust and long-term partnerships.

So to all the aspiring Level-Funded brokers out there, I say this: don't be afraid to take the high road. Don't compromise your values for the sake of a quick sale. And don't let the unethical actions of others discourage you from doing what's right. Instead, focus on honing your craft, deepening your knowledge, and delivering exceptional results for your clients. Surround yourself with like-minded professionals who share your commitment to integrity. And never lose sight of the fact that your success is ultimately measured not just by the numbers on your balance sheet, but by the lives you touch along the way.

If you do that—if you stay true to your principles and always put your clients first—then I have no doubt that you will thrive in this business. You'll build a book of business that is the envy of your peers. But more importantly, you'll go to bed each night knowing that you made a real difference in the world, one client at a time.

The Cost of Fraud

Before concluding this book, I have a few more words on fraud:

If you recall from the Philosophy of Insurance section in Chapter 2, trust is an essential ingredient for any system that attempts to balance risk to work. Fraud not only steals from the pockets of the innocent, it pilfers the currency of trust that binds society together. Without trust, all that is left behind is a trail of suspicion and skepticism. In short, fraud exacts the highest toll on the integrity of good people.

The Coalition Against Insurance Fraud estimates that insurance fraud in the US alone costs tens of billions of dollars annually. While most of this is perpetrated through federal programs like Medicare and Medicaid—simply because they're the largest targets—fraud, waste, and abuse in the private health insurance space is still estimated to account for around 15% of total costs.

To put that in perspective, if the average American is paying $400 per month for their health plan, $60 of that is being siphoned off to cover the misdeeds of the one out of 100 people who are committing fraud. It's a staggering tax on the honest majority, and it erodes the very trust that is essential for the insurance system to function.

What's worse is that the perpetrators of fraud often feel justified in their actions. They rationalize that they're simply getting what's owed to them, or that the system is rigged anyway so they might as well get their piece of the pie. But this mentality is corrosive. It eats away at the social contract and makes everyone more suspicious and less willing to participate in good faith.

And it's not just the policyholders who are guilty of fraud. Sadly, some of the biggest offenders are the healthcare providers themselves. There have been cases of hospitals calling in a second surgeon for a procedure just so they can bill for two providers, even though only one was needed. Or submitting claims for high-cost medications that were never actually administered to a patient.

These providers often cloak their actions in a veil of righteousness, claiming that they need to pad their bottom line to keep the lights on and serve the community. But in reality, they're just gaming the system for their own financial gain, and eroding the trust that is essential for the healthcare system to function.

As a broker, you have a critical role to play in combating fraud, waste, and abuse. It starts with being vigilant in your underwriting and claims monitoring, and not being afraid to ask tough questions or demand documentation when something seems amiss. But it also means being a vocal advocate for transparency and accountability, and working with your carrier and TPA partners to root out bad actors and send a clear message that fraud will not be tolerated.

It's not an easy battle, and it's one that requires constant vigilance. But it's a fight worth fighting. Every dollar lost to fraud is a dollar that could have gone toward lowering premiums, expanding coverage, or improving patient care. And every instance of fraud that goes unchecked erodes the trust that is the bedrock of our industry.

Remember, the vast majority of people are honest and play by the rules. They're counting on us to be their watchdogs and their advocates, and to create a level playing field where everyone has a fair shot at getting the care they need at a price they can afford. That's the promise of health insurance, and it's a promise worth fighting for.

So as you build your book of business, make a commitment to being part of the solution rather than part of the problem. Hold yourself and your clients to the highest standards of integrity, and don't be afraid to speak out when you see something that doesn't pass the smell test. It may not always be the easiest or most popular path, but it's the only way to build a sustainable and ethical business in the long run.

THE TRIPLE BOTTOM LINE

As a young, hustling health insurance agent, it's easy to get caught up in the grind of prospecting, quoting, and closing deals. But amidst the hustle, it's important to pause and reflect on the deeper purpose behind your work. Selling health insurance isn't just a way to make a living—it's an opportunity to simultaneously build a rewarding career, help your clients' businesses thrive, and make the world a little bit better in the process. That's the triple bottom line.

I was reminded of this higher calling during a recent meeting with a new client, a small manufacturing business I had just brought on board with a Level-Funded plan. The owner, visibly moved, shared with me how one of his long-time employees had suffered a severe accident a few months prior. The injuries were extensive, requiring emergency surgery and weeks of rehabilitation.

"I was so scared we were going to lose him," the owner confessed. "He's not just an employee to me—he's like family. And I knew that if he couldn't get the care he needed, or if the medical bills bankrupted him, it would devastate not only him but all of us."

Thankfully, because of the Level-Funded health plan we had put in place, this valued employee was able to receive top-notch treatment at a renowned trauma center without having to worry about the financial fallout. The plan covered the vast majority of his expenses, allowing him to focus on healing and eventually return to work. And because the group had a relatively healthy year overall, the company still received a small surplus check at the end of the plan year.

As I listened to this story, I was struck by the profound ripple effects of my work. By crafting a smart, sustainable health plan for this small business, we hadn't just saved them money—we had potentially saved a life and preserved the livelihood of a beloved team member. Those plan dollars had kept hope in their hearts during one of the darkest times imaginable.

This is the essence of the triple bottom line. When we do our jobs with excellence and integrity, we create wins for ourselves, our clients, and society as a whole. We build profitable practices that provide for our own families and futures. We help small businesses gain a competitive edge by attracting and retaining top talent with first-class benefits. And we contribute to a healthier, livelier workforce and economy by ensuring that hard-working Americans have access to the care they need to thrive.

Of course, achieving this triple bottom line is easier said than done. It requires not only technical expertise in plan design and risk management, but a deep commitment to putting people first in all that we do. It demands that we look beyond the next sale to cultivate long-term relationships. And it challenges us to think creatively about how we can use our unique skills and resources to make a meaningful difference in the lives of those we serve.

But when we get it right—when we align our own interests with those of our clients and our communities—the results can be extraordinary. We can help small businesses not only survive but thrive in an increasingly competitive landscape. We can give hard-working employees and their families the peace of mind that comes from knowing they're protected during life's toughest moments. And we can play a vital role in building a more just, compassionate, and prosperous society for all.

As an old mentor of mine used to say, "Life is too short to sell something you don't believe in." And I wholeheartedly believe in the power of Level-Funded health plans to make a real and lasting difference for small businesses and their people. I've seen firsthand how this innovative model can bend the cost curve while improving access to care. I've witnessed the joy and relief on clients' faces when they receive those surplus checks. And I've been humbled by the stories of lives touched by the plans we've put in place.

I encourage you to keep the triple bottom line front and center as you build your own practice. Don't just focus on hitting your quotas or padding your commissions. Create genuine value for your clients, your community, and yourself with every plan you design and every relationship you forge.

It won't always be easy. There will be long days and sleepless nights, difficult conversations and daunting obstacles. But when you stay true to your values and keep your eyes on the prize of the triple bottom line, I promise you the juice will be worth the squeeze. You'll build a book of business that not only pays the bills but fuels your passion. You'll earn the trust and loyalty of clients who see you not as a vendor but as a partner in their success. And you'll go to bed each night knowing that you're using your talents to make a real difference in the world.

That's the promise and the opportunity of the Level-Funded Revolution. It's not just a smarter way to finance benefits. It's a chance to fundamentally redefine the role of the broker as a catalyst for positive change.

Now, I know this high-minded talk of purpose and impact can feel a bit daunting, especially when you're first starting out and just trying to keep the lights on. It's easy to fall into the trap of thinking that you need to be some kind of saint to make a real difference. But the truth is, positive change often starts with small, consistent actions that compound over time.

Consider the story of two pottery classes proposed by art historian Robert J. Sternberg. One class was told they would be graded solely on the quantity of pots they produced, while the other was told they would be graded on the quality of a single pot. At the end of the semester, which class do you think produced the better pots?

Surprisingly, it was the quantity class. While the quality class spent all their time theorizing about the perfect pot, the quantity class was busy churning out pot after pot, learning from their mistakes and gradually honing their craft. And in the end, all that practice led to mastery.

The same principle applies to building a purpose-driven benefits practice. You don't have to start with some grand, world-changing vision. Just focus on being a little bit better each day than you were the day before. Make one more call, send one more email, read one more article on innovative plan design. And most importantly, treat each client interaction as an opportunity to learn, grow, and add value. Over time, those small actions will start to add up. You'll gain confidence and expertise, develop a reputation for excellence, and attract more and more clients who share your commitment to doing well by doing good. And before you know it, you'll look up and realize that you've built not just a successful business, but a meaningful legacy.

IN DEFENSE OF OUR SYSTEM

As we come to the end of this book, I want to leave you with one final thought. The American healthcare system, for all its flaws and frustrations, is still the engine that drives medical innovation for the entire world. It's the reason we have cutting-edge treatments, lifesaving drugs, and ever-improving standards of care that benefit humanity as a whole.

Yes, our system is imperfect. Yes, it can be confusing, expensive, and at times maddening. But it's also the system that has given us the polio vaccine, heart transplants, and gene therapies that were once the stuff of science fiction. It's the system that attracts the best and brightest minds from around the globe to push the boundaries of what's possible in medicine. And it's the system that, for better or worse, subsidizes research and development that improves health outcomes for people in every corner of the planet.

As a proud American, these numbers give me solace. Our country, with just 4% of the world's population, is responsible for over 90% of all new drugs and medical devices brought to market each year. We are quite literally saving and extending lives on a global scale, thanks to the incentives and opportunities created by our market-driven approach to healthcare.

Now, I'm not saying our system is beyond reproach or that we shouldn't strive to make it better. Of course we should. There are still too many Americans struggling to access or afford the care they need. There are still perverse incentives and entrenched interests that put profits ahead of patients. And there are still gaping disparities in health outcomes based on race, income, and geography that we must work tirelessly to close.

But as we grapple with these challenges and debate the best path forward, let's not lose sight of the incredible good that our system makes possible. Let's not be so quick to throw the baby out with the bathwater in pursuit of some idealized notion of perfection. And let's certainly not cede ground to those who would seek to dismantle the very engine of innovation that has driven so much progress for so many.

Instead, let us approach reform with a spirit of humility, pragmatism, and appreciation for what works. Let us recognize that the solution to what ails our system is not to tear it down, but to build upon its strengths while addressing its weaknesses. And let us embrace our role as brokers, advisors, and advocates in shaping a healthcare future that is more accessible, more affordable, and more equitable for all.

That is the task before us. That is the challenge and the opportunity of our time. And that is why I am so passionate about the work we do as health insurance professionals. Because in the end, this isn't just about selling policies or managing risk. It's about using our unique skills to change and save lives.

It's about making sure that the single mother waiting tables can take her kid to the doctor without fear of going bankrupt. It's about giving the aspiring entrepreneur the freedom to pursue her dreams without worrying about how she'll pay for her insulin. It's about ensuring that the researcher on the brink of a breakthrough has the funding and the incentives to see it through to fruition.

This is the noble calling of our profession. This is why we get up every morning and fight the good fight, even when it feels like an uphill battle. Because we know that what we do matters. We know that every plan we design, every client we serve, every innovation we champion has the potential to make a real and lasting difference in someone's life.

So as you go forth and build your own practice in this crazy, complex, ever-changing world of health insurance, never lose sight of that bigger picture. Never let the day-to-day grind dim the fire of your purpose. And never, ever stop believing in the power of what we do to change lives for the better.

The American healthcare system may not be perfect, but it's ours to shape and to steward. It's ours to defend and improve. And it's ours to leverage as a force for good in the world, one client and one community at a time.

That is the legacy I hope to leave behind. That is the legacy I hope you'll help me build. And that is the legacy that will make all the long days, sleepless nights, and hard-fought battles worth it in the end.

So go ahead and make it happen. Embrace the Level-Funded Revolution with all your heart and soul. Fight for what you know is right, even when it's hard. And never stop believing in the power of what we do to make a difference.

The future of healthcare is ours to write. Let's make it a story worth telling.

Want to Learn More?

Continue your education here with deeper insights, reviews, and production tools.

ACKNOWLEDGMENTS

"Do not pray for easier lives. Pray to be stronger men."
—*John F. Kennedy*

This work, and the work we do at American Trust Administrators, would not be possible without the decades of innovation preceding us. I look with gratitude to the Old Cowboys of the industry, specifically my father. I hope to honor the work they have done that allows Main Street to continue to have a shot in this marketplace.

We stand on the shoulders of giants. We do not think ourselves tall. We only know that we are needed to continue a task, even if we know that our betterment is required. We are what is left to carry the mantle.

To Thomas Stein Sr., Hobson Carroll, Steven Schouweiler, and Ralph Weber for their contributions to this book, and to the many other Old Cowboys who have helped pave the way, thank you for being examples of what stronger men can be through lifelong careers of service.

Additionally, I would like to thank Andy Earle, Ray Pendleton, Nancy LeGere, and Jud Spencer for their input and guidance in the creation of this book. Thank you, Jud, especially for keeping me out of trouble.

About the Author

Thomas Stein is the CEO of American Trust Administrators. His early exposure to the health insurance industry came through his father, Thomas Stein Sr., with whom he made his first sales call in eighth grade. Committed to continuous learning, Thomas dedicates a significant portion of his day to reading and connecting with agents to better serve their needs. He travels extensively to engage with brokers, emphasizing the importance of personalized communication and long-term client relationships. Thomas, a self-described dealer in hope and knowledge, lives in Kansas City, KS with his wife and sons.

The Great Life Calculator

If you are patient, you can build a great life. The road might seem long at first given the amount of work you'll need to put in upfront, but on the timeline of your career this is a small investment. Hustling today for relationships that can last years, if not decades, is well worth the time saved each year after. Please keep in mind that retention rates change, but as a bit of info: great brokers retain 90% of their business whereas poor brokers retain less than half.